Life Coaching

An Introduction

By - Tony Nutley

Copyright © 2022 UKCPD

ISBN: 9798835225460

First Edition

Published by The UK College of Personal Development

All Rights Reserved - The book may not be used for commercial purposes without written permission.

No part of this book may be reproduced in any form, printed or electronic, without permission from the author.

UK COLLEGE OF PERSONAL DEVELOPMENT

www.ukcpd.co.uk

www.ukcpd.co.uk

www.ukcpd.co.uk

TABLE OF CONTENTS

Chapter One: A History of Coaching
The role of the Coach

Core Coaching Competencies

Chapter Two: The Development of the Life Coach
The Personal / Life Coaching Industry Today

The Differences Between Personal Coaching, Life Coaching, etc.

The Life Coaching Process

Chapter Three: Communication - The Key Skill
A model for understanding communication

Chapter Four: Why Coaching Works
The Generative Coaching Cycle™

The forming of new habits

Qualities required for good coaching

Chapter Five: The Wheel of Life - A Starting Point
Power Coaching Questions

Chapter Six: Coaching Models
The WHAT Coaching Method™

The GROW Model

The APROCESS Coaching Model

Chapter Seven: Developing Your Practice
Exploring different coaching niches

Business development options

Review

www.ukcpd.co.uk

www.ukcpd.co.uk

This book is in no way a template or training to become a coach. Rather, it's a selection of some of the key content we teach on our various coaching programmes.

All suggestions made in this book are for guidance only, a skilled coaching professional will be able to apply this guidance in a way that fits with their practice and client base.

Remember, to be a credible and confident coach, we always suggest you undertake a *recognised and accredited* coach training programme.

For additional information on the options available, simply visit our website: www.ukcpd.co.uk

Chapter One: A History of Coaching

The concept of coaching has been around for as long as the human race itself. Right from the earliest days the older or more skilled taught the young how to hunt, cook, paint pictures on cave walls and just how to be useful and effective members of their tribes or communities in general.

This type of practical, skill-related coaching still exists in most societies to this day. However, a more sophisticated form of coaching, aimed at inspiring greater understanding or awareness can be seen emerging in the earliest philosophies and religions, ranging from the lessons incorporated into cultural fables to the lessons incorporated in the biblical parables.

Throughout history and literature there are examples of coaching in action but surprisingly the practice (at least in terms of executive development and who had even heard of Life Coaching till the late 90's) appeared to fall into disuse in the late twentieth century. These were the days of the full-blooded management training programme. It's not that long ago when most management development programmes lasted at least five days.

The major British management training colleges advertised general 'open programmes' to which managers and executives from all walks of life and business would come to be put through a pre-set and unalterable programme irrespective of their individual needs. In the USA programmes were often considerably longer and the five to eight weeks 'total executive development experience' was not uncommon.

This approach to development was not without its merits and the author of this book has experienced and been involved in such forms of training and has seen it bring about immediate benefits to those being trained. But there are problems inherent in this approach and they are both economic as well as more subjective in nature.

The economic issue became apparent with the downturn of the economy in the 1990s when the organisations that had hitherto supported lengthy 'open programmes' found that they could no longer afford to go down this costly route and started to demand more tailor-made solutions from training providers.

This initially took the form of requiring customised programmes that were aimed at addressing specific organisational issues as opposed to the more general 'sheep dipping' approach.

At the same time both organisations as well as their managers started to see the benefits of a more individualised approach to personal development. This is mirrored in society where we have gone from a situation based on the collective where the emphasis was on community and the nation, to one focussed on the individual where we all have to manage our own careers and lives.

While generic skills could be taught, there were a host of issues ranging from complex to highly personal or confidential matters that demanded something other than training. People needed something that enabled issues to be discussed in depth and solutions arrived at by debate, reflection and discovery over a period of time. This was in stark contrast to the pre-packaged solutions so typical of most training programmes.

But coaching still took time to catch on. In the late 1990s one of the authors - a leading executive coach - was asked what he did for a living. He replied with some pride that he was an executive coach. "Oh so you take people to the seaside?" came the reply.

The coach initially thought that the other person was teasing him and was just about to compose a sarcastic reply when he saw to his amazement that the question was genuine. What made it even more amazing was that the questioner was a senior HR professional.

Since then, things have moved on.

As the idea of coaching developed, organisations started employing psychologists to understand employee motivation and development needs, as well as for recruitment, selection and assessment. Sport also had a strong influence on the rise of coaching.

Tim Gallwey's book "The Inner Game of Tennis" in 1974 related to a more psychological approach to peak performance. He stated that the opponent in one's head was greater than the one on the other side of the net.

In 1992, Sir John Whitmore, a motor racing champion, published "Coaching for Performance" where he developed the most influential model of coaching - the GROW model (goal, reality, options, will). We will explore this model in detail later in this book. Gurus such as Stephen Covey and Antony Robbins also fuelled the appetite for personal development and awareness.

In the 1990's the US went into recession and corporate downsizing became the rage. It may have seemed good in theory but did not take account of human needs. This left managers and leaders in highly stressed environments without support, which in turn added to the need for individuals and organisations to continuously develop. This need for performance maximisation has also contributed to the upsurge in coaching.

The industry has also changed from one where coaches were brought in as often for poor performers as for high performers (often dealing with performance issues where the manager did not want the hassle or conflict) to today, where the vast majority of coaching is aimed at high level performers rather than remedial cases. What's more, the rise of Life Coaching today is becoming accessible to all walks of life, not just top performers.

Many large private, public and voluntary sector organisations (as well as small and medium sized businesses) use executive coaching as a standalone development solution or dovetail coaching with other organisational development programmes.

The Role of the Coach

Executive, business or performance coaching can be simply described as helping someone to learn in order to improve their performance. It is usually a one-to-one activity and is not about issuing instructions but is about helping, showing, giving feedback, explaining and encouraging.

Coaching recognises that most development takes place on the job and that often real learning requires a demanding task or problem to be tackled.

The process requires regular and effective contact between coach and client and a recognition that all sorts of occasions - ranging from a change in the coachee's job to gearing up for a specific project - may require this sort of intervention.

Coaching recognises that the coachee already has the vast majority of answers/facts and the coach's role is to stimulate that knowledge/learning and allow the coachee to unlock and achieve their true potential.

As a coach, leader or manager it can be as simple as asking your colleague one single question so they can engage their brain and learn. One question is all it takes for the coach to be inspirational.

The Six Roles of an Executive Coach

At the International Coach Federation European Conference in Italy in 2003, Robert Dilts ran a seminal session titled 'From Coach to Awakener'. He stated that coaching is the process of helping another person perform at the peak of his or her abilities.

It doesn't presuppose that people are broken - on the contrary, it helps them identify and develop their strengths. It starts from the assumption that people have the answers, and that the coach's role is to help that person to overcome internal resistances and interferences, give feedback on behaviour and give tips and guidance.

But Dilts added that a coach plays five further roles:

Guiding and Caretaking

Guiding is the process of directing another person along the path leading from where they are presently to where they want to be, providing a safe and supportive environment without unnecessary distractions or interference from the outside.

Teaching

Teaching relates to helping a person develop cognitive skills and capabilities and the emphasis is on learning. It focuses on the acquisition of general skills, rather than on performance in specific situations. A teacher helps a person to develop new strategies for thinking and acting.

Mentoring

A teacher instructs, while a coach provides specific behavioural feedback, in order to help a person, learn or grow. Mentors, on the other hand, guide us to discover our own unconscious competencies, and strengthen beliefs and values, often through their own example.

www.ukcpd.co.uk

Sponsorship

Sponsorship involves creating a context in which others can act, grow and excel. Sponsorship is about the development of identity and core values, awakening and safeguarding potential within others. It involves the commitment to the promotion of something that is already within a person or group, but which is not being manifested to its fullest capacity.

Awakening

Awakening goes beyond coaching, teaching, mentoring and sponsorship to include the level of vision, mission and spirit. An awakener puts other people in touch with their own missions and visions and thus the coach needs to know his/her own vision and mission and purpose.

Core Coaching Competencies

The following list of Core Coaching Competencies is taken from a longer list issued by the Association for Coaching and illustrates just some of the key areas of knowledge, skills and behaviours that are generally required of a coach.

Knowledge: As a coach you need to know...

- What the coaching process involves
- What models of coaching can underpin your role as a coach
- What personal and professional capabilities the coachee needs to develop
- How to manage the coaching relationship
- How to set boundaries
- How people learn and how to adapt to different learning styles

Skills: As a coach you need to be able to...

- Listen and communicate at different levels

- Ask searching questions
- Influence with integrity
- Give feedback without causing offence
- Be empathetic
- Demonstrate confidence in oneself and also the coachee
- Facilitate goal setting
- Be challenging and yet compassionate
- Always act with integrity and in the best interests of the coachee

Behaviours: As a coach you should...

- Encourage self-discovery
- Act as a role model
- Be non-judgemental / Use humour appropriately
- Illustrate that you value diversity
- Show tact and awareness
- Always maintain confidentiality
- Seek to build the client's confidence and self-esteem
- Show other sources of support to client
- Critically evaluate one's own effectiveness

For additional information simply visit the Association For Coaching website: www.associationforcoaching.com

Chapter Two: The Development of the Life Coach

In time the ideas contained in popular personal development books and the awareness of executive coaching began to take root in the general public's conscious and the idea of a "Life Coach" quickly took a foothold in the options individuals looked at when considering personal and professional development.

Various individuals and organisations have added to the ideas, concepts and published material on Personal or Life Coaching and have promoted these with varying amounts of success. However, one man stands out as having made the biggest constitution to the ideas and practice of Life Coaching, Mr Thomas Leonard.

One Man's Powerful Influence On Personal / Life Coaching

Thomas Leonard was the driving force behind developing and educating the world about the personal coaching process. Thomas came on the scene from the financial world in about 1988, where he had a life-planning course entitled "Life Creates Your Life." "Leonard is credited with codifying coaching into a curriculum to teach people how to be a coach and that could be taught globally, even taught telephonically, in the early days of coaching."

It's been said that Leonard worked as a synthesizer working with "hundreds, thousands of people to create his coaching format and to develop ideas and attitudes that added to his work.

He also had in his vision, a vision of himself being highly impactful, being a leader, and being competitive against other companies doing similar things. He was intensely competitive and intensely collaborative at the same time, various commentators credit Leonard with popularizing codifying, and globalizing the discipline of coaching.

Leonard's background is business, specifically finance, where he was working for Werner Erhard and doing life planning on the side. Leonard, and others such as Laura Whitworth and John Whitmore, took some basic ideas and applied their business background to creating an industry that is called coaching.

Thomas and his partners created the personal coaching process to fulfil the one human void that none of the other major human improvement processes (see below) would even touch.

Thomas created a new human improvement process that assisted people to discover and unravel the mystery of themselves. The greatest mystery in the world is not global warming, nor whether there is life on another world, no, it's us, how we see and understand (or not) ourselves.

This new human improvement process called personal or life coaching works exceptionally well to assist you to clearly, quickly, completely, and confidentially discover yourself, without any hint of judgment or guilt. With your personal coach, you will become the World's Leading Expert on you. The greatest form of human improvement and growth is self-awareness.

The personal coaching industry has grown exponentially since 1992, because personal coaching works so well, and because of Thomas Leonard's vision, and his energy. Personal coaching has evolved into a viable and recognized industry because personal coaching accomplishes the exceptional goals it was designed to achieve.

Generally, we (The UK College of Personal Development) do not believe that enough people fully understand the possibilities and the universal ramifications and multiple uses of the personal / life coaching process. Maybe Thomas did, and that might be why he was such an outspoken advocate of personal coaching.

Thomas travelled extensively coaching, speaking, and training wherever he could. He captured the imagination of many people to persuade them to become joint pioneers in this new process.

I never met nor spoke with Thomas Leonard. He died of natural causes in February of 2003, before I had the chance. From what I gather, Thomas was a real character with strong beliefs and was prone to contradictions.

Thomas tangled with a number of people whom he felt were competitors.

For this reason, some people still have a difficult time acknowledging Thomas Leonard's real contributions to personal coaching. Likewise, he was a great inspiration and supporter to many others, who still champion his contributions.

The Personal / Life Coaching Industry Today

Estimates seem to indicate that there are between 30,000 to almost 80,000 people calling themselves coaches today. Approximately 12,000 to 20,000 are added each year. Those wishing to engage a coach have a vast number of coaches to pick from, the "best coach for you" can live almost anywhere, as many coaches work with their clients over the telephone or via Zoom.

Right now, anyone today can call himself or herself a life coach. There are no rules, regulations, laws, restrictions or enforced codes. Because of the many successes of personal coaching in the beginning years, many people have jumped on the bandwagon to take advantage of the good name personal coaching created.

Yet, these many different people calling themselves coaches now offer different coaching methods, styles, philosophies, structures, ethics, backgrounds, niches, and purposes.

The coaching community itself is also confused about how to determine what the coaching process is. The various bodies that claim to represent the coaching industry and its members offer many definitions of coaching, some of which contradict each other based on an influence by organizational philosophy, practitioner backgrounds, theories, and models."

Additionally, most definitions assume an absence of serious mental health problems in the client and that coaching's purpose is to affect some kind of change using similar knowledge, skills, and techniques.

The Life Coaching industry is not perfect! We estimate that fewer than 20% to 30% of the people who call themselves "coach" are actually qualified and delivering coaching services similar to the personal coaching process designed by Thomas or fits into what the leading professional bodies would recognize.

The good news is that this is changing, FAST. The main professional bodies are now working together to set minimum standards in training, membership and the insistence on an ongoing CPD programme and supervision.

The Differences Between Personal Coaching, Life Coaching, Business Coaching, etc.

Thomas Leonard named his new human improvement process "Personal Coaching." Because "personal" coaching is very personal. The other titles for "personal" coaching did not appear on the scene until about 10 years later, beginning with the label "life" coach. In 2002, a TV show "Starting Over" created two characters and called them "life coaches" even though their actions and the personal characteristics they exhibited had no relationship to the "personal" coaching process created by Thomas Leonard.

Instead, the show took advantage of the personal coaching process that had grown in popularity because it worked so well.

But this fictional TV had a very strong influence, especially on the mainstream media who adopted the term "life" coach because one of their own (another Hollywood produced TV program) had coined the phrase and process. Today the term "life" coach is more often associated with the "personal" coaching process.

In the UK today the Life Coaching industry has grown exponentially, the main bodies that represent coaches and inform the public are:

The Association For Coaching - AC

www.associationforcoaching.com

The International Coaching Federation - ICF

www.coachfederation.org.uk

European Mentoring and Coaching Council – EMCC

www.emccouncil.org/uk

There are of course many, many other smaller niche organisations, however, the three named above represent the mainstream in coaching and its development in standards etc and they are working together to create a provisional framework to make Coaching a legal title** and professional career.

Many believe this will become a reality in the next few years. The UK College of Personal Development will of course keep

www.ukcpd.co.uk

all its students and graduates up to date as the guidance and requirements develop.

(**this has happened to Counselling and Psychotherapy in 2012)

The Ten Major Human Improvement Processes

The ten most popular human improvement processes are shown below in alphabetical order:

- The life coaching process
- The consulting process
- The education process
- The mentoring process
- The psychiatric process
- The self-help process
- The spiritual process
- The teaching process
- The therapy process
- The training process

The Life Coaching Process

Life coaches focus 100% on you achieving your chosen future coaching goals. Life coaches are equal partners and are not your superior. Coaches assist you to improve and grow as a person as the means to achieving your goals. Life coaches assist you to become the "World's Leading Expert on You" by providing you very objective, clear, and very confidential perspectives about you, so you see and understand yourself better than ever before. You, the client is the expert.

Your life coach focuses on you discovering and unravelling the mystery of you to find and understand the powerful person you really are. You discover information within you, versus learning information outside you. Life coaches encourage and hold you accountable to take the actions you select as necessary to achieve your goals. Life coaches concentrate on you actually implementing (executing) what you know to achieve the goals you want.

The consulting Process

Consultants are recognized experts in their fields, who either sell their expert advice or perform their expert actions (or both) to complete a task on your behalf. Consultants are hired to solve problems for you. These problems are always external to who you are. Consultants will rarely affect your personal improvement. Some examples of consultants are attorneys, doctors, auto mechanics, and accountants.

The Education Process

Educators focus on you learning certain external information or concepts. They involve themselves in your learning process to be sure you grasp the information or concept being conveyed. Generally, educators are experts in their fields, but not always. Educators will focus on you improving your knowledge, your understanding of concepts and your ability to learn.

The Mentoring Process

Mentors focus on providing you sage advice and wisdom gathered through experience and knowledge when you ask for their insight. Mentors can be considered a library of human knowledge in the particular areas of life they have gained expertise. Mentors normally focus on providing knowledge, understanding and direction, but have been known to help in your improvement as a person when you allow yourself to become the subject.

The Psychiatric / Therapy Process

Psychiatrists are Medical Doctor experts who focus on helping you to overcome mental and thinking imbalances. They provide drugs and behaviour change methods to adjust your mental activities back to as normal as possible. Psychiatrists focus exclusively on you improving as a person to get better control of your thinking and emotional activities.

The Self-Help Process

People who use the self-help process try to perform many of the other human improvement process by themselves.

They usually follow the advice of self-help books, Television shows, tapes, seminars, radio shows, and/or Internet sites. When using the self-help process, you must provide the guidance, energy, support, wisdom, and direction to learn and do what you feel is necessary to accomplish your goals. You may act as your own teacher to train yourself, to become the expert to solve your problems, by acting as your own consultant.

The self-help process also requires you to conduct most if not all of the improving processes alone. It will normally take much longer to accomplish objectives using the self-help process than if you use any of the other people supported improvement processes listed above. Using the self-help process normally produces an incomplete process.

It has been reported that the average person reads only 16 pages of a self- help book. The what, the why and the how are undoubtedly all provided for practically any subject, but the actual execution without the help of other people is much more difficult than it appears. It's apparent that people need other people to actually grow and improve as a person.

The Spiritual Process

Spiritual people focus on helping you to relate to another force or higher power outside you. They help you discover and follow a known or even new belief system of values to guide you in your moral and or spiritual actions. Usually, spiritual leaders are considered experts, and practice some form of Religion, whether self-created or as part of an established Religion. They focus exclusively on you improving as a person within the structure of the spiritual beliefs (Religion) followed. Priests, rabbis, pastors, or mullahs are considered spiritual leaders.

The Teaching Process

Teachers focus on providing you external information, data or concepts. Teachers are experts in their field. You are responsible for absorbing the information provided, so you will become more knowledgeable. Teachers also do not necessarily focus on improving you as a person. Teachers will not do the learning for you.

The Therapy Process (talking therapies)

Therapists focus on helping you overcome past problems that impede your ability to function in a normal day to day manner. Therapists direct you to revisit past events to discover and resolve conflicting issues that have burdened you. Therapists are experts in their field. Therapists direct their sole attention on you to resolve internal conflicts that will affect your personal improvement. A typical conflict therapists will help clients resolve is overcoming mistreatment by parents.

The Training Process

Trainers focus on teaching you how to perform something. Trainers are experts in their fields and teach you various processes, methods, and or skills, to do something in a predetermined manner. Trainers do not necessarily focus on you improving as a person.

Trainers instruct you on what to do and how to do it. You might use a trainer to learn how to operate a particular computer program, how to operate an aeroplane, or how to hit a golf ball.

Why Be a Life Coach?

Coaching is a rich and rewarding career. Coaching helps many people. Here are three typical types:

1. People who want to succeed, whether at work or in love. They are sometimes held back, whether through fear, timidity, or procrastination.
2. People who feel stressed out, often by their work. Many want to spend more time with their family or spouse. Others want to down-shift and lead a simpler life.
3. People who feel something is lacking in their life, whether a community or just time for themselves. Coaches can help them change their priorities.

As you can see, people want change in their lives. But they don't know how to achieve it. Sometimes they don't know what changes they want. As a coach you can help them unravel their concerns and point them in a new direction or their own choosing.

The Growth of Stress

A survey of 650 GPs who have practised for more than 15 years reveals that society has become much more stressed. The survey, which was published in the British Medical Association News Review, shows that:

- 80% of GPs said the number of patients seeking help for stress related problems has increased significantly over the period.
- 58% said their patients were drinking more. Half blamed stress for the rise.
- Nearly half said they are making more psychiatric referrals than they were in 1979.

The survey paints a picture of a nation in which people are weighed down by stress, young adults find it difficult to cope, marital problems are resolved by divorce, and elderly people are increasingly left to fend for themselves.

This survey, like many others, shows that people really benefit from coaching and that coaching is being recommended by more and more GPs.

How Coaching Compares with Counselling or Therapy

Coaching is much newer than therapy or counselling. But many therapists are adding coaching to their repertoire because it is so popular.

Therapy and counselling are essentially for people who are unwell. Whereas coaching is for well people who need guidance.

As a coach, you must be aware of the possibility that sick people (whether mentally or physically unwell) will ask you to coach them. For their sake and for yours, you should get them to seek qualified advice.

Your job, as a coach IS NOT to provide answers. Let me repeat that. You don't provide answers. Why? Because clients don't do what people tell them what to do with their lives, and if they did, then coaching is not for them.

Imagine if you did give them specific advice and they followed it, and then it turned out to be a personal disaster, guess who is going to get the blame?

Coaching clients are just like everyone else, they do only what they want to do. So, until they have decided to quit their job or move to Alaska, there is nothing you can do to persuade them of that, no should even have in mind to try. Coaching is about asking questions, not telling individual what to do!

So, what is the Role of the Coach?

It is to:

- Help clients understand themselves
- Help clients prioritise their lives
- Facilitate change by being a sounding board
- Challenging a client's beliefs and self-image by asking powerful questions
- Help the client see the alternatives

Not having to provide answers has an added bonus. It means you don't have to know the answers to the client's problems. For example, you don't have to be a financial expert. And this isn't a cop-out. It's important not to get too far into the technical detail of the client's problems. Most of life's important issues are simple: it's making the decision that's hard.

Nevertheless, we do guide people into achieving change. And when a client reveals what they want, we'll push them into achieving their goal. But that isn't the same as telling them what to do.

Different Approaches to Life Coaching

There are four main types of Life Coaching in popular use today:

1. Telephone Coaching
2. Face to face Coaching
3. Email Coaching
4. Zoom Coaching

Telephone Coaching

Telephone coaching is the main method used by coaches. In fact, when coaches talk about 'coaching', they mean 'telephone coaching'.

Telephone coaching does away with the wasted time spent travelling or waiting for a client to arrive. Neither you nor your clients have to dress up or have the house tidy for your coaching. And you don't have to fight traffic.

But most importantly, it lets you coach people in distant places who would otherwise never be able to receive coaching from you. When people think of coaching, they assume that it involves face-to-face discussions. This is perhaps because therapy is usually conducted in this way. But this isn't the case for coaching.

In some countries, primally the USA, coaching is predominantly conducted by telephone. And during the phone conversation, most clients feel that you are there with them. For although the phone conversation is business-like and methodical (on your part) it is also charged with emotion because you're discussing with the client things that they don't reveal to anyone else.

Typically, telephone coaching involves two, three or four telephone calls a month. A typical programme involves three telephone calls a month. The calls are usually 30-45 minutes in length. You need to tell your client how long they will get and publicise the information in your brochure or on your website.

Some coaches offer a range of options, from two to four calls a month. The cost of two calls a month is depended on the local market and the marketing skills of the coach. If you choose three calls a month, you can put the meetings at weekly intervals, on for example the 3rd, 10th and 17th. This leaves the client with a week free (the 24th) before starting again at the 3rd.

You can also offer unlimited telephone coaching, this is for the wealthier client for whom money is no object. You should also

www.ukcpd.co.uk

allow the client to phone you when necessary for extra sessions.

The investment costs mentioned above is for guidance only, you will decide the value of your service and you will be able to sort out what the market can afford. Decide whether you will offer telephone coaching or not, think about the kind of price you will charge for your service and be sure to do some research on local coaches via the internet first. This is often a useful guide.

Later in this book we discuss how to price and design your services. Some coaches allow unlimited emails during the coaching period. This is a good idea when you are getting started. But when you get busy, amend your terms for new clients, so that they can pay a little extra for a month's unlimited email support.

Face to Face Coaching

In-person sessions are suitable only for people who live in your area. This might limit your marketplace if you do not wish to travel to other locations. For this reason, Life Coaching is so often carried out over the telephone.

Face-to-face coaching has many advantages. You get to meet the client in person, and so you can see their body language. You can hear the gaps between words, and because you have more clues, you can more readily understand what the client is really trying to say.

Later, we will consider whether you should meet in the client's home or your own, or in some other place such as an office. Each of these has its merits. Once a client has had a program of four face-to-face coaching sessions, they may decide, if prompted by you, to opt for a further programme of tele-coaching or Zoom Coaching. This lets them unburden themselves, and tell you, their progress. It also lets you gently encourage them to stick to their resolutions and maintain progress towards their goals.

Therefore, tele-coaching or Zoom Coaching may be important for the client. If you cut them adrift after a program of face-to-face coaching, it is easy for them to slip back into their old ways. This approach helps to keep them moving their life forwards. The considerations regarding price, frequency and duration of in-person coaching is the same as for telephone coaching.

E-mail Coaching

Like the telephone, email allows coaches to operate far beyond their town or city. It also allows you to continue coaching people after they have left your locality, or when they are at college or on a business trip.

Email coaching is often used as an extension of telephone coaching. For example, you might let a client send you unlimited emails (each one of which you need to reply to). You undertake to reply within two days (or you may choose a different period).

Email works well for clients who feel happiest behind a keyboard. It could also involve you sending them weekly lessons on how to achieve their goals. Sometimes coaches offer stand-alone email coaching. This involves an unlimited number of emails passing between the client and coach each week. At the end of the week, the coach may summarise what has been discussed.

You can also set up a more structured system. You get information from the client about their problems and concerns, and regularly email them about their progress in these areas. The emails will ask questions and seek responses and will thus help the client to achieve change.

www.ukcpd.co.uk

The downside of a pure e-mail coaching system is that there is so much lost in the communication that there is face-to-face coaching or even telephone coaching. E- mail can be cold and the power and warmth of both the questions and the responses can be lost.

Zoom Coaching

Online video calls via Zoom or other video calling services have become a super popular option as like Telephone Coaching it opens up the opportunity to have coaching clients in just about any part of the world.

The advantage of Zoom Coaching over Telephone Coaching is, of course, you can see the client and they can see you, clearly for many a better option.

Understanding Yourself / Coaching Client's Map of The World

Coaches need to understand their own feelings. Every coach is human and unwittingly carries their own prejudices or worldview. Coaches often come from a similar class, race, age and educational attainment.

Thus, a white, male, middle-class coach will have certain preconceptions towards women or certain ethnic minorities. Let's take a look at the cartoon views often promoted by the tabloids as an example, how do you feel about the following groups:

- The French
- The Germans
- People who vote for the opposite political party from you
- People who live in council houses
- The working class
- The elderly

www.ukcpd.co.uk

- People who hold opposite religious views to you
- Racists

As a coach, you will encounter clients with extreme views. Your job is not to have a political or economic argument with them, but to find out what their problem is. Often, a client's difficulties or problems cause them to hold extreme views and is what brings them to coaching in the first place.

Coaching and Outcomes.

Within the coaching knowledge base and various approaches there is one thing that they all agree with, there has to be a CLEAR, ACHIEVABLE, RESOURCED and AGREED outcome for the client. Having a nice chat is NOT coaching, that is simply having a nice chat.

There are various models, GROW, CREATE, APROCESS, PESEO, etc, in this book we will explore 3 models.

Chapter Three: Communication - The Key Skill

I guess it is pretty obvious, to be a great coach, you need to be a great communicator. There are many models on communication, this is the NLP Model:

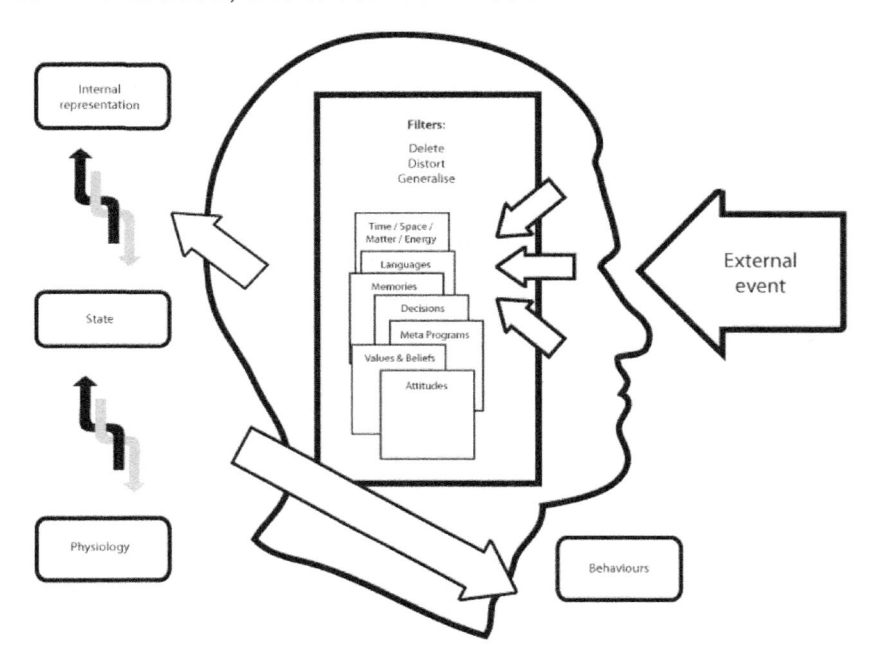

This is useful as it clearly set out the different processes that happen as we endeavour to communicate and to gain rapport with our clients. Essentially, gaining a powerful rapport is about developing the skill of mirroring the client's model of the world back to them. What we mean by this is, matching body language where appropriate, matching their tone of voice and especially their language.

From the field of NLP, we know that most of us have a preference in the use of and hearing of specific linguistic predicates or to put it another way, for a specific channel of communication. The main channels are:

www.ukcpd.co.uk

- Visual
- Auditory
- Kinaesthetic
- Non-Specific or Digital

Some examples are given below of linguistic predicates that may indicate the types of thinking processes that the speaker is using. By matching these predicates or channel of communication you can build rapport and gather more information from the speaker.

Visual

'I see what you mean...' 'I get the picture...'

'Things are looking good...'

'Can you show me what you mean...' 'We need to focus on this aspect...' 'He has a bright future here...'

'You have added some sparkle to your presentation...'

'I had an insight into how things look from his perspective...

Auditory

'I like the sound of that...'

'We have a very harmonious working relationship...' 'Your idea really struck a chord with the boss...'

'I like to listen to my team's ideas...' 'I hear what you say...'

'I'm getting into my rhythm with the job now...' 'He told me the relevant details...'

'I'd like to discuss how things are going...'

Kinaesthetic

'I like the feel of that ...'

'I have a sense of what you mean...' 'He's got his finger on the pulse...'

'I'm trying to give some shape to these ideas...' 'Things are really moving now...'

'I'm under a lot of pressure at times...'

'I like concrete ideas I can really get to grips with...' 'He's very hot on quality control...'

Digital Phrases

In regard to your concern

We are considering the following possibilities an interesting dilemma.

A viable solution

As we analyse the potentiality Consider the options

Value quality

Promote a philosophy.

So, the trick is to really listen to the actual words they are using and to match it as much as you can.

To be able to develop this skill you need to really practice, over and over. Once you master this your skills as a coach will really shine through.

Some people may also use all of the modalities; they are often the ones who are thought of as 'naturally good communicators'.

For more information on how NLP can be a useful set of tools in coaching please ask a member of the UKCPD team.

www.ukcpd.co.uk

Why coaching Works.

There are many reasons why coaching works where other interventions seem to either not work so well or take a lot longer to have a lasting and noticeable effect.

The first is that coaching is all about the client, for the time set aside for the coaching session, the client has the total attention of the coach, and this time is focussed on exploring, challenging, listening and reflecting and of course goal setting with the client's agenda in being centre stage.

Think about it going through life with the right set of plans and advice. Coaching can take years off the time it would have taken to reach your goals!

What follows are considered by some to be the top 7 principles of why coaching works:

1. Builds Self-Confidence. When you're following the direction of someone successful following their lead your goals can be obtained faster and with less trial and error.

2. Guided Plan. Sure, you can draw up an action plan alone, but when you create your plans with the help of a coach, you know your plan is practical and it will work. A coach will know shortcuts and keep you on target.

3. Struggles. Coaches help clients deal with your current difficulties and tensions in their life and business. They also know techniques to avoid similar situations in the future.

4. Individual Attention. Coaching offers one-to-one attention, so the client is guided along your chosen path avoiding the pits in the road. If the client runs into problem, the coach will be there to give support and guidance.

5. Handling Challenging Situations. Even with a great plan, sometimes things will get off track. When you run into an obstacle, the coach can help the client face up to the situation and direct you back on a proven track. You will feel more comfortable realizing that you're receiving skilled and practical advice.

6. Flexibility. The client is in control of how you would like to use your coach. Do you want assistance with short-term or long-term goals? Perhaps you need help in both areas. Whatever it is, you're the one in control of the situation.

7. Passion. A coach will be passionate about their work; it's their enthusiasm and passion that rub off on you. Sometimes it's hard to keep up with their drive. But inspiration is one of the essential reasons why coaching will always endure.

The truth is that while the above may tick the box for many, the reasons why coaching works are far more interesting, effective and are more complex by far. This is demonstrated in the number of books written on the subject and the number of different models that have been developed to work in different areas of human endeavour.

Chapter Four: The Coaching Process

All of the above said, there is a widely agreed format to the coaching process. The following model helps us see just how this powerful process works.

Looking at this model it's easy to see a natural flow of the coaching process, given the correct tools and attitude a good coach can guide their client through the different stages of the process and help them set and achieve their outcomes successfully.

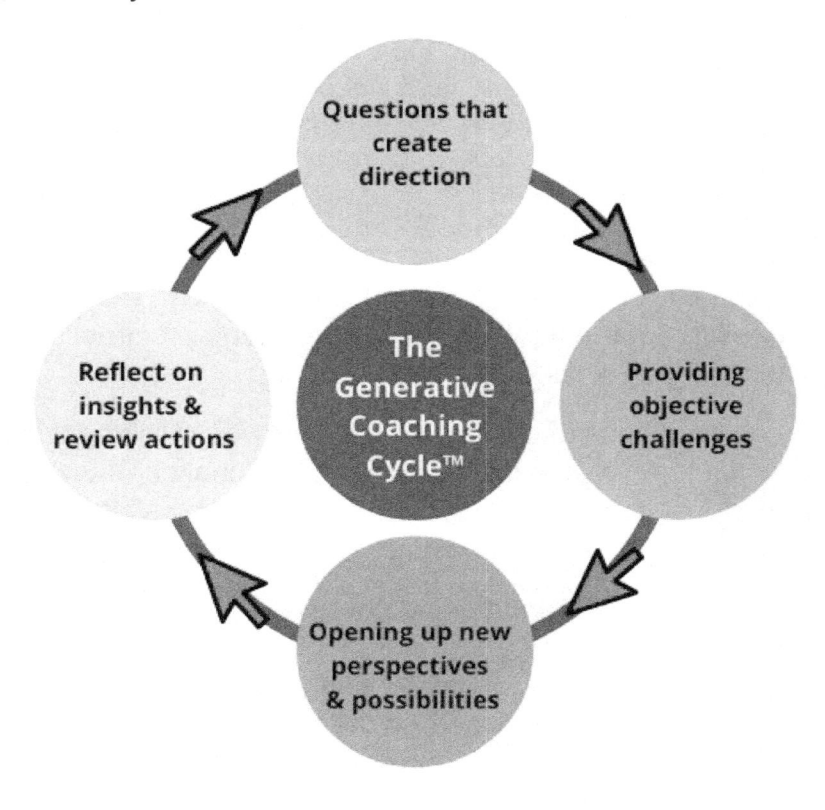

The Generative Coaching Cycle™

For those not familiar with the Generative Coaching Cycle™, it is the idea that generally, a coaching session involves a four-stage process that follows the following course:

1. Questions to create a direction.
2. Provide objective challenges.
3. Open new perspectives and possibilities.
4. Reflect on insights and commit to taking action.

Looking at this model it's easy to see a natural flow of the coaching process, given the correct tools and attitude a good coach can guide their client through the different stages of the process and help them set and achieve their outcomes successfully.

Questions help create direction by focusing our attention on a specific key area, the type of question, of course, will depend on client to client but the point is clear asking the right question at the right time helps the client get direction by focusing on a specific area of their life.

The questions of course will then provide challenges because within the questioning process we will challenge the clients' responses. We will hear things like limiting beliefs or Phrases like I can't or it's not possible or it's not possible etc.

Now within this questioning process what begins to happen is we begin to open up new perspectives for the client, this includes new ways of seeing things and new opportunities to take steps forward based on the insights from the challenging questions that we're asking the client.

Lastly of course within the session, we reflect on the process and say things like: so what have we got from this, session what specific actions are you going to take and of course we encourage the clients to reflect and take note of any new insights that they've had.

Coaching means supporting someone in reaching their goals. The Life Coach may or may not help define those goals (most often will be involved in this process) but once they are set, it is the coach's job to support, empower, encourage and challenge their client to fulfil those goals and to be the best they can possibly be.

The easiest way to visualise this is to look at the example of an athletics coach. The coach is not the one who runs the race. He is not the one who puts in the long hours of training, with the goal of winning Olympic gold. That's the athlete. The coach is the one who:

- Is also at the track at 6 a.m. (Motivation)
- Has his stopwatch ready to time the athlete and chart his/her progress. (Assessment)
- Shouts encouragement from the side-lines. (Support)
- Gives advice on performance, based on his knowledge, experience and observations. (Guidance)
- Highlights areas for improvement – what the athlete can do better. (Challenges)
- Points out areas of excellence – what the athlete does well. (Feedback)
- Provides everything the athlete needs to be able to concentrate fully on his/her performance. (Empowerment)

A good Life Coach highlights their client's behaviour, talents and their shortfalls. Every one of us has abilities which we think are normal; those things we do naturally, easily, which we assume everyone else can do. When we make such assumptions, we sell ourselves short.

A good coach will correct that. The coach will make sure their clients see how good they really are. Similarly, a coach will bring to awareness the areas which can be improved too, in order for the client to become a better version of themselves.

We are reliant on others to point out certain behavioural traits to us. The coaching relationship is an ideal place for that kind of feedback. Without such appropriate feedback, our blind spots remain just that, and our behavioural patterns remain unchanged.

Once we become aware of our behaviour, the next step is to change the aspects which need changing. And this is where we come across one of the most important and most fascinating aspects of the Life Coach's work. All we have to do is see our own behaviour.

All we have to do is see what other people have been seeing for days, weeks, months, even years. Because once we see it, the changes and transformations are already taking place. There is no need for any additional effort.

There is still the need for awareness, focus, discipline and application (here, again, we see the same kinds of words we hear in connection with top-class athletes). But there is no need to make any extra effort to change your behaviour. You know where you are, and you know where you want to be.

This is the magic that you as the Life Coach brings to the relationship, to see what has not been seen and to reflect it back to the client. The development process starts in many ways from this point forward.

The Forming of New Habits

When we try a new approach, it often doesn't work the first time around; when we try to establish new patterns of behaviour we often fall back into old habits. It's at these times that a coach becomes invaluable because he will remind you why you started this journey; the coach will remind you of your goals and of how enthusiastic you were at the beginning.

So, you as the Life Coach will tell and also show your clients just how far they have come, what real progress they have made. We all know from experience that it is only too easy to lose sight of or underestimate the progress we have made, so it is the coach's job to remind clients where they were and show them where they are now. Point out the evidence, what can be seen, heard and felt!

It's clear that there are good reasons why all top sports men, women and teams have coaches. To be successful, they need someone to be straight with them, to guide them, provide constructive and critical feedback, to challenge their patterns of behaviour and create more successful habits.

They need someone to show them what they are doing well and also what they can do better; someone to show them how good they are and, when things are not going so well, to remind them why they started and what they set out to achieve.

It's the same for the general population, and the job of the Life Coach is to be that person!

Qualities Required For Good Coaching

Coaching is unlike training, consultancy, advising, or providing a professional service in which work is completed on behalf of a client. The qualities required for good coaching are different to those found in these other disciplines too:

Listening

In coaching, listening is more important than talking. By listening, people can be helped to overcome their fears, be offered complete objectivity and given undivided attention and unparalleled support. This leads to the intuitive questioning that allows the client to explore what is going on for themselves.

Communication skills

Coaching is a two-way process. While listening is crucial, so is being able to interpret and reflect back, in ways that remove barriers, pre-conceptions, bias, and negativity. Communicating well enables trust and meaningful understanding on both sides.

Coaches are able to communicate feeling and meaning, as well as content - there is a huge difference. Communicating with no personal agenda, and without judging or influencing, are essential aspects of the communicating process, especially when dealing with people's personal anxieties, hopes and dreams.

Good coaching uses communication not to give the client the answers, but to help the clients find their answers for themselves.

Rapport-building

A coach's ability to build rapport with people is vital. Normally such an ability stems from a desire to help people, which all coaches tend to possess. Rapport-building is made far easier in coaching compared to other services because the coach's only focus is the client. When a coach supports a person in this way it quite naturally accelerates the rapport-building process.

Motivating and inspiring

Coaches motivate and inspire people. This ability to do this lies within us all. It is borne of a desire to help and support. People who feel ready to help others are normally able to motivate and inspire. When someone receives attention and personal investment from a coach towards their well-being and development, such as happens in the coaching relationship, this is in itself very motivational and inspirational.

Curiosity, flexibility and courageous

Coaching patterns vary; people's needs are different, circumstances and timings are unpredictable, so coaching relationships do not follow a single set formula. Remembering that everyone is different and has different needs is an essential part of being a coach. Ultimately, everyone is human - so coaches take human emotions and feelings into account.

And coaching is client-led - which means that these emotions have to be tapped into from the very beginning of the coaching process. So, having the flexibility to react to people's differences, along with the curiosity and interest to understand fundamental issues in people's lives, are also crucial in coaching.

The coach's curiosity enables the client's journey to be full and far-reaching; both coach and client are often surprised at how expectations are exceeded, and how much people grow.

All this does take some courage - coaches generally have a strong belief in themselves, a strong determination to do the best they can for their clients, and a belief, or faith that inherently people are capable of reaching goals themselves.

Life coaches come from all backgrounds

Life coaches and personal coaches come from all kinds of backgrounds and professions. Not surprisingly, coaches tend to like people, and many coaches come from 'people' and 'caring' professions.

Coaches come from backgrounds as varied as these, and the list is certainly not exhaustive:

Teaching	Complementary Therapies
Nursing	Human Resources
Management	Personal Trainers
Consulting	Voluntary workers
Prison Service	Charity workers
Therapy	Armed forces
Counselling	Emergency services
Training	Service industries

And many people in business, institutions, management, and organisations of all sorts learn how to become coaches so as to enrich their existing roles with the very special skills, methodologies and philosophies that coaching entails.

Becoming a coach fosters the coach's own personal growth

Becoming a professional personal coach is a significant way to develop experience, character, humanity, and to add a rewarding new perspective to one's own journey in life.

Typically, seeking a new outlook on life, a willingness to learn, and a passion for helping other people are the first steps in the process towards becoming a coach.

Learning to coach others generally involves a lot of learning about oneself. Coaches almost always find that they have had to explore and resolve a number of new personal issues themselves, before they are ready to begin helping others to do the same. Some of this experience can be surprising; it can also be a little scary, but it is usually ultimately rewarding.

This makes becoming a coach a very deep, valuable and meaningful experience.

Learning to be a coach is a serious step and a serious commitment. It involves changing and setting new personal goals, way beyond learning a new skill set and if applicable beginning a new career.

Personal Development of The Life Coach

Given what we have just covered, at this point in your learning it's a good idea to review your personal and professional goals in a clear well and well thought out and structured way.

Chapter Five: The Wheel of Life - A Starting Point

So, there are many ways to start the coaching process, one way is the use of the Coaching Wheel tool.

It's one of the most tools commonly used by professional life coaches, it helps clients consider each area of their life in turn and assess what's off balance.

And so, it helps identify areas that need more attention. We suggest that you carry out the following exercise as a "self-coaching" experience to enable you to have a real sense of how this works.

The Wheel of Life

The Wheel of Life is powerful because it gives you a tool to help your clients create a vivid visual representation of the way their life is currently operating, compared with the way perhaps they would rather it to be.

It is called the "Wheel of Life" because each area of the client's life is mapped on a circle, like the spoke of a wheel.

I suggest you complete this exercise for yourself as you read this section just so you get the feel for just how useful this can be as a tool for focussing on key areas for starting a coaching / change process.

Here is an example:

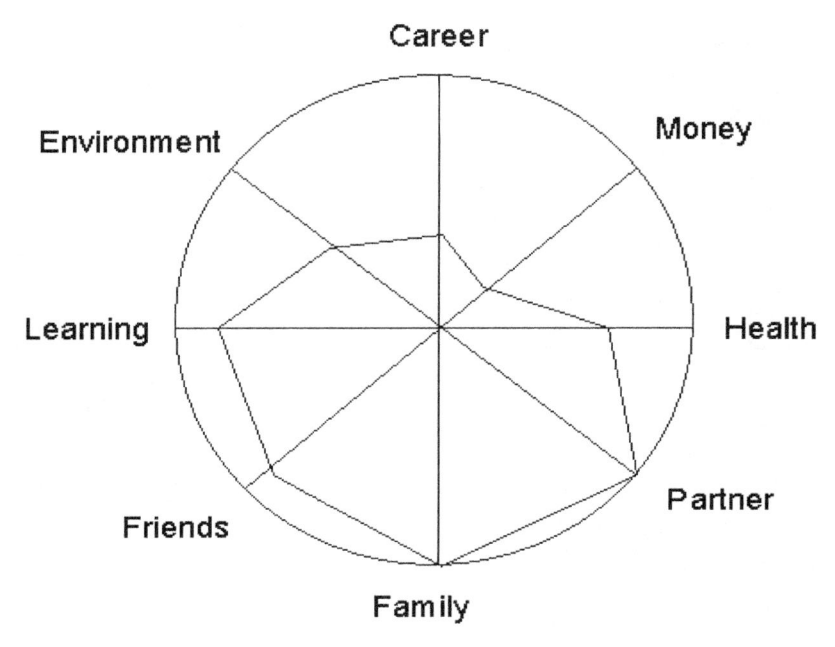

Wheel of Life diagram with spokes labeled: Career, Money, Health, Partner, Family, Friends, Learning, Environment.

1. Start by brainstorming the 6 to 8 dimensions of your life that are important for you. Different approaches to this are:

The roles you play in life for example: husband/wife, father/mother, manager, colleague, team member, sports player, community leader, or friend.

Areas of life that are important to you for example: artistic expression, positive attitude, career, education, family, friends, financial freedom, physical challenge, pleasure, or public service.

Your own combination of these (or different) things, reflecting the things that are your priorities in life.

2. Write down these dimensions on the Wheel of Life diagram, one on each spoke of the life wheel.

3. This approach assumes that you will be happy and fulfilled if you can find the right balance of attention for each of these dimensions. And different areas of your life will need different levels of attention at different times. So, the next step is to assess the amount of attention you're currently devoting to each area.

4. Consider each dimension in turn, and on a scale of 0 (low) to 10 (high), write down the amount of attention you're devoting to that area of your life. Mark each score on the appropriate spoke of your Life Wheel.

5. Now join up the marks around the circle. Does your life wheel look and feel balanced?

6. Next it's time to consider your ideal level in each area of your life. A balanced life does not mean getting 5 in each life area: some areas need more attention and focus than others at any time. And inevitably you will need to make choices and compromises, as your time and energy are not in unlimited supply!

7. So the question is, what would the ideal level of attention be for you in each life area?

8. Plot the "ideal" scores around your life wheel too.

9. Now you have a visual representation of your current life balance and your ideal life balance. What are the gaps? These are the areas of your life that need attention.

10. And remember that gaps can go both ways. There are almost certainly areas that are not getting as much attention as you'd like. However, there may also be areas where you're putting in more effort than you'd ideally like. These areas are sapping energy and enthusiasm that may better be directed elsewhere.

11. Once you have identified the areas that need attention, it's time to plan the actions needed to work on regaining balance. Starting with the neglected areas, what things do you need to start doing to regain balance? In the areas that currently sap your energy and time, what can you STOP doing or reprioritize or delegate to someone else? Make a commitment to these actions by writing them on your worksheet.

You can use the Coaching Wheel as preparation for goal setting, for yourself and your clients, a first step on the road to personal change if you will. It helps identify the areas you want to work on and is a great way of visualizing your current and desired life. Once you are working on improving your life balance, it's also a useful tool for monitoring your life balance as it changes over time.

The Coaching Wheel is a great tool to help you improve your life balance. It helps you quickly and graphically identify the areas in your life to which you want to devote more energy, and helps you understand where you might want to cut back. The challenge now is to transform this knowledge and desire for a more balanced life into a positive program of action. And this is where the skill of the Life Coach comes in.

You can download a free Life Coaching Wheel from our website: www.ukcpd.co.uk/lifecoachintro

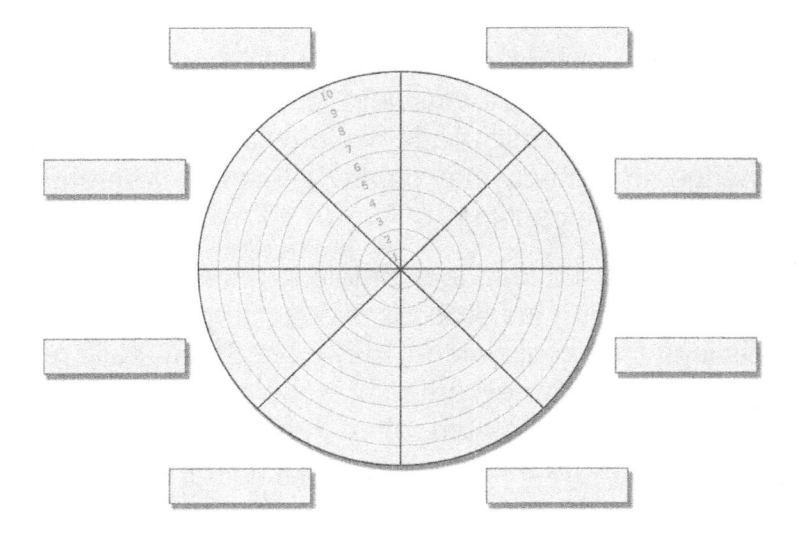

www.ukcpd.co.uk

Power Coaching Questions

Powerful questions are part of the foundation of life coaching – sending the client to places within their imagination and their previous experiences; places of introspection, creativity, light bulb moments; questions that are demanding and that the client might not ask often, if ever ask themselves.

But such questions can't exist in life coaching without powerful listening – the two come together as a package. Powerful listening is more than just hearing the client's words and interpreting them. It's about hearing the rise and fall of the words, the pitch and tone, the volume and the pauses between the words. It's often about using one's instincts to hear what is really being said. Such listening enables questions to be well framed, relevant and hit the spot effectively.

Powerful questions often make the life coaching client pause and reflect purposefully. By their open-ended nature they enable the client to open up. They are never 'why' questions, which usually make people defensive, sometimes shutting them down rather than opening them up. '

Powerful questions may seem simple, and they are – to pose, but not necessarily to answer – but they help to create ways to self-explore and elicit your own new answers and bring about change. In this way they create self- empowerment a key benefit of life coaching.

There exists the idea that certain types of questions are really good at starting the process of coaching, what we mean by this is at first, an individual may never have really reflected on their lives, and as a starting point so called Power Questions are a good place to start, often these questions are given to a client along with a Coaching Wheel before their first meeting with the coach.

Take some time to reflect on the following pages of Power Questions, notice where these questions take your thinking and what that may or may not mean to you as you think about your personal future.

Which questions seem to have more of an impact? What is the reason for this? The questions are divided into four sections:

1. A Starting Point
2. Preparing for Action
3. Gaining New Perspectives
4. General Review & Diagnostic Questions

What follows is a set of questions you may weave into your coaching session:

Power Coaching Questions (A Starting Point)

If you were to FULLY live your life, what is the first change you would start to make?

What areas of your life could be upgraded/ tweaked?

What could we work on now that would make the biggest difference to your life?

How would you feel about doubling that goal?

What are you tolerating or putting up with in your life?

What do you want MORE of in your life? (Make a list)

What do you want LESS of in your life? (Make a list)

What are three things you are doing regularly that don't serve or support you?

How could you make this goal more specific or measurable?

What would be the biggest impact from achieving your goal(s)?

www.ukcpd.co.uk

What would you try right now if you knew you could not fail?

How can we make this something you're aiming towards, rather than something you're trying to move away from?

What in your life do you love?

What in your life do you hate?

What's one thing you would love to do before you die?

Is now the right time for you to make a commitment to achieving these goals?

What has to happen first?

What could we work on right now that would really put a smile on your face?

For your life to be perfect, what would have to change?

What do you really, really want?

What's one change you could make to your lifestyle that would give you more peace?

When was the last time you did something new for the first time?

Prepare For Action Stations

What's the first/next step?

What research could you do to help you find the first (or next) step?

Who could you talk to who would illuminate this issue?

Who should you be hanging out with – so that achieving this goal becomes natural? (i.e., who's already doing it?)

How can you get the knowledge/information you need?

What are three actions you could take that would make sense this week?

On a scale of 1 to 10, how excited do you feel about taking these actions?

What would increase that score? (e.g., handle fear, clearer steps, more support, more fun)

To quote Tony Robbins, what would "massive action" look like?

What will happen (what is the cost) of you NOT doing anything about this?

Gaining New Perspectives

What can you learn from this?

In what way is the current situation absolutely perfect?

How could you turn this around immediately, and enjoy the process?

What in this situation can you find to be grateful for?

What are you doing well? What can you do better?

What's one way you could have more fun in your life?

What is the value of your current attitude?

What's your favourite way of sabotaging yourself, and your goals?

What should I say to you if I spot you doing this?

Who can you ask to be this support for the future?

When specifically, will you begin this journey?

What evidence will you accept that you are making progress?

General Review & Diagnostic Questions

What are three of your greatest strengths?

What are you most excited about now? What are you looking forward to?

What's one way to get more energy into your life?

If your relationship was IDEAL, what's one thing that would be different?

What would be your ideal career – if you could do anything?

What's one thing that you could do to give yourself more peace financially?

What is your life really about? What is your purpose?

If you had to guess your life purpose (from looking at your life to date), what would it be?

What would you like most to be acknowledged for so far in your life?

Who in your life should be acknowledged more?

Would you like to acknowledge them for something today?

What are you specifically going to do differently now?

Remember, the above is NOT a script, rather these questions are a prompt and a guide as you begin your coaching skills and confidence.

You can download a free Power Coaching Questionnaire from our website: www.ukcpd.co.uk/lifecoachintro

Chapter Six: Coaching Models

There are many coaching models, in fact, it's safe to say that there are probably as many coaching models as there are people practising coaching, and that's a good thing. In fact, a many-models approach is probably your best bet to lead people towards finding the best solution possible.

What is a coaching model?

A coaching model is a framework, it does not tell you how to coach but rather it's the underlying structure that you can use when you're coaching someone. It's like having a high-level strategy that allows you to "see the battlefield," therefore increasing your ability to respond adequately to whatever coaching situation you're faced with.

Learning from different coaching models has definite value, as no one model has all of the answers to all of the challenges you'll be faced with as a coach.

Why are there so many coaching models?

Coaching integrates many fields of knowledge, so it's likely that many theories and models were adapted for coaching. This also means that you have a broader base to learn from. Having many models available can actually help you if you decided to codify your own personal way of working as your experience grows.

What do most coaching models have in common?

Most coaching approaches share some things in common:

- The establishment of a relationship that's built on trust, unfeigned communication and confidentiality.
- The formulation of client-based, agreed-upon goals and expectations.

- A deep questioning and learning dynamic in relation to people's goals.

By learning and understanding each model's commonalities, you can then integrate and effectively create your approach.

In this book, we will look at a selection of models; try them out for yourself and see what seems to work for you and your clients. Of the three coaching models that we are looking at in this book, the second last has gained a key place in the coaching cannon of printed books. The GROW model.

We will also look at an NLP model in detail as I believe it is a simple yet powerful approach to setting goal, or as we say in NLP, Well-formed Outcomes.

So, let's start to explore some coaching models, we start off with The WHAT Coaching Method™.

The WHAT Coaching Method™

I originally developed the WHAT Coaching Method™ as a training drill for students studying to become qualified professional coaches.

It was super useful as it helped the students focus on the client's outcome by keeping them away from getting too involved in the client's story which often seemed to happen when asking HOW, WHEN, WHERE, and even WHY questions.

However, since the early development phase of the idea, it has grown and developed into a model of sorts with its own merits. The approach seems to keep the client highly engaged in the coaching process and focus their energies on WHAT they actually, what this outcome would do for them (the goal beyond the goal).

The WHAT? Coaching Method™

- Step One. What do you want?
- Step Two. What's the current situation?
- Step Three. What strategy ideas can we generate?
- Step Four. What time frames are we looking at?
- Step Five. What actions will you commit to?

During the process, they also explore the key reasons for making the decision to make a change in their situation, asking WHAT has been the trigger to engage a Coach has been a powerful point in the process as it helps the client reflect on the situation and gain clarity on the direction they really wish to work towards.

Then developing a strategy to ensure actions and overall success, we explore key areas including the resources required to enable the client to actually begin the journey.

Lastly, a key time frame is agreed upon, and we clarify the first step and then get a commitment to taking it ASAP!

When used skilfully, it generally ensures the criteria for the NLP concept of Well-Formed Outcomes are met, the criteria for NLP Well-Formed outcomes are:

Want to = motivation:

> The client must believe that the goal is achievable.

How to = means:

www.ukcpd.co.uk

> The client must have or develop the realistic knowledge of the physical & mental steps necessary to achieve the goal.

Chance to = opportunity:

> The client requires the resources to put the strategy into effect and have the ability to deal effectively with interference, blocks, and resistance that are going to happen.

Agreed Evidence = assessment of progress:

> The client needs to be clear on the evidence of progress, sensory specific evidence (See, hear, feel) which enables clients to really focus on the progress they are making towards their desired change and future outcome.

The last few years of using this approach both within our training college (UKCPD – www.ukcpd.co.uk) and with my own clients it's become really clear that the WHAT Coaching Method has become more than a starting point in training for generating a powerful questioning style, it can be an excellent coaching methodology to get the best for your clients.

Building on our foundational coaching model, the Generative Coaching Cycle™, the WHAT questioning approach really does help clients gain clarity on their outcome and the strategy to achieve success.

Unlike other coaching models, the WHAT Coaching Method™ is not an acronym but an emphasis on variations of just one question – WHAT?

To give you an overview of how this works, consider the general flow of most coaching models, let's use GROW model as most people who have looked at the coaching process are familiar with this approach.

G – Goal – What do you want?

R – Reality – What's the current situation?

O – Options – How can you move forward- a strategy for success etc

W – Will – What will you actually commit to doing etc?

What I noticed was that both coaches and clients often got bogged down way too much detail, often off topic around the exploration of the reality and the development strategy by asking HOW, WHEN and even the worst of all coaching questions, WHY!.

That is how and why I developed the idea of just asking WHAT questions.

So, given this general coaching session flow mentioned above, let's now look at the framework I have been working with clients and our students using the WHAT Coaching Method™.

Remember, these are sample questions, in a real coaching session, flexibility and creativity are key.

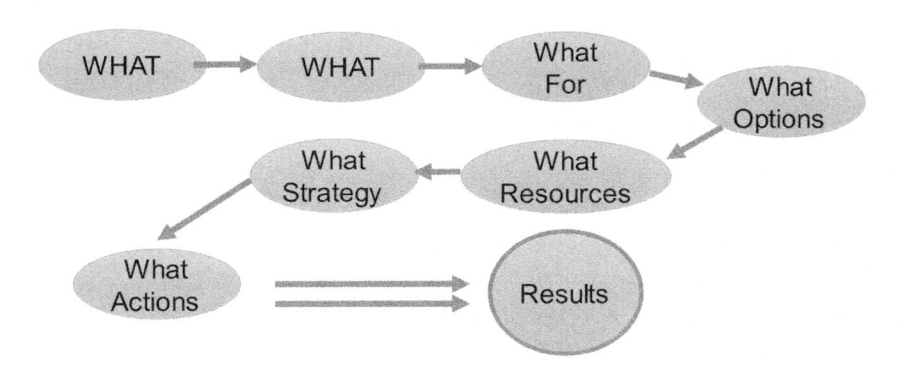

WHAT → WHAT → What For → What Options → What Resources → What Strategy → What Actions → Results

www.ukcpd.co.uk

Step One - What do you want?

What's the current situation?

What's prompted the need for change?

What else?

What would you rather have?

What would your ideal outcome be?

What does that look like?

Thinking about all we have explored, what outcome are we going to focus on in this session?

What level of importance on a scale of 1 to 10 will you give this outcome?

What's the impact of not achieving this outcome?

Tell me in one sentence, what will achieving this outcome do for you?

What else?

Step Two - What's the current situation?

Ok, so what's going on right now, describe the current situation.

What effect is this having on you?

What has triggered you to seek out some support in making a change?

What other factors are contributing to this issue?

What part if any are you playing in this dynamic?

What is it about this situation that really needs to change?

What strategy or solutions have you tried to improve the situation?

What will happen if you do not make a change?

Step Three - What strategy ideas can we generate?

What resources will it take (think, time, money, people etc) to get this done?

What resources do you already have? Skill, time, enthusiasm, money support etc?

Let's brainstorm some strategy options, let's explore as many options as we can in the next few minutes.

What is your first idea?

What else?

What else?

Looking at all the options, what seems to be the best option right now?

What is the first step in getting this outcome started?

What do you believe has prevented you from getting this in the past?

Step Four - What time frames are we looking at?

Reflecting on all we have covered, what time frame are you going to work to?

What's a date take you can commit to right now?

What one thing can you do today to get the ball rolling?

Step Five - What actions will you commit to?

Okay, so what is the very first step to take to make this happen?

www.ukcpd.co.uk

What evidence (see, hear and feel) will you contract with both me and yourself that will indicate you have:

> A, made a start?
>
> B, are halfway there?
>
> C, you have successfully achieved your outcome?

What is the number one thing you got out of this session?

What clarity have you got out of this session?

Example: The WHAT Coaching Method™

Here we have an example of The WHAT Coaching Method™ being used, this is a transcript taken from a LIVE training session at UKCPD.

Coach: Okay. So, what would you want from this session?

Client: Um, I want to encourage my boss or my boss to be more trusting of us as a team, I find it really difficult cause he questions us all the time.

Coach: Tell me that again.

Client: I want my boss, my boss to be more trusting of me and my team. He comes in and he questions every decision and action all the time.

Coach: And what is it about these questions that makes you feel or enables you to think that he's not trusting you? What is about the questions?

Client: Um, he sometimes asking me why I made that decision Um, he's asking me lots of why questions and I feel work quite a high performing team. And I feel that it's, if he trusted me more and the team, he wouldn't need to ask those questions.

So, I feel there's a lot of, we have to prove ourselves at the moment.

Coach: So instead of him asking why questions, what would you run that he was doing that would help support you and your team?

Client: I would like him to assume that we're doing it. And then the, I will report back if there were any issues or any concerns.

Coach: What do you think you could do to start that process of him backing off?

Client: Um, I think I could perhaps generate a report or give him regular updates so that he's reassured, and I've started to do a bit of that now. Yeah.

Coach: What else?

Client: I think the next step is to build a better picture for him as to how we're perceived by our business that we support, um, because he doesn't work in the same location as us. So, he's quite removed from those customers. So, I think it's important to give him a better picture.

Coach: so, a report, what else?

Client: Yes, actually, I think I need to say to him, it's really unhelpful when you do.

Coach: Okay. So given those options, what do you think you're actually going to do?

Client: I want to do the last option, but I don't want to offend, because I've tried the other two.

Coach: What way could you deliver that message to ensure he's not offended? And he really gets a sense of what is you're trying to do specifically?

Client: I could perhaps say that, although we welcome his involvement and that's a really nice thing that perhaps there's an element of him being too, of him being too involved. And perhaps actually, if he could help us to, um, change some of the areas that we struggle with, um, I would like him to focus on those.

Coach: What can you do to ensure that the conversation you have keeps that outcome and doesn't go off.

Client: Um, that is a challenge because he tends to veer off as do I. Um, but, um, I thought, um, maybe I could create a list of what I'd like him to action. And this is, this is my issue, or this is my concern. Usually when you have an appraisal from your boss, you put in, oh, I'm going to achieve so-and-so by this time, I'm kind of asking him to achieve something by this time.

And it's that shift. And it's how he'll respond to that. So, it's the coaching up.

Coach: Yeah, we have talked about that before.

Client: Yeah. Yes.

Coach: Okay. Given your experience and because you mentioned it before, what angle do you think would be good to spin it so that he sees this as a positive that look up. So, you look empowered, so we're doing this as an example.

Client: Yes. When he knows I'm doing this now. Um, so, um, one of the things I could do is say, okay, would you mind if I try something, I learned something at the weekend. Would you mind if I tried this and let me know if it changes, you know, the outcome.

Coach: Okay. So again, we've looked at some options, you've kind of a sense of a strategy to how you might be going to do this.

What do you think might not work out? What what's the full, safe here that you think? Uh, what's plan B as well asking.

Client: Plan B would be that we present it as a collective team. So that he appreciates, it's not just my viewpoint. It's actually a collective viewpoint. It's not just my perception. It's the perception held by several others. But I've been asked to be the person who speaks up and says about it.

Coach: So, thinking about all of that, that you've said the options, strategy plan B. What are you actually going to do?

Client: I'm going to write a list of what he wants to action, um, how it would benefit us as a team, how we can inform quicker as a result. Um, and I'm also going to write a list of what we do and what I feel we do well and what we don't need guidance on, because he can assume that

www.ukcpd.co.uk

it's being taken care off. Um, and I'll also, um, use me as an escalation point.

If he feels he isn't being taken care of, then we'll have, uh, an update a particular time and date.

Coach: And, um, what sort of timeframe are we talking about?

Client: Um, I'll try and instigate. Well, I think I'd have the conversation with him before Easter. So, I'm on leave next week. So, I'll have the conversation when we're back.

Coach: Super, um, thinking about where are you right now, do you think there's anything else that you might want to - - Uh, uh, what if, what if, what if or are you pretty clear abouts what's going to happen?

Client: I think I'm; I think I'm pretty clear. The key is keeping the focus going in there with a strategy, um, which I hadn't really though. So, um, but I've got a clear idea of that. Um, it overall it will make him look really good. If we deliver all of this because he's our overall manager. Um, and it will also allow him to go back to his boss and say, hey, look, this is what the team suggested. It was a different approach but look at how it worked.

Coach: So, given what you've just said, that sounds really positive. What else can you and your team do that were really have impact? So he goes, wow.

Client: I guess at work; we use a term called sell the benefits. So, we can sell the benefit of us trying this way and what it will do for our customers and what it will do for him regarding how he's perceived and how he he's

www.ukcpd.co.uk

perceived as a manager actually. And he'll, um, it will come across that he is actually managing us without him needing to manage us.

Coach: Wow, that sounds really great, okay. Hold that thought, we will stop here.

So, I think it fairly clear how just asking WHAT questions focuses the attention of the client, so they generate options for moving forward.

So, why not ask WHY questions you are probably asking. Well, because every time you ask why, invariably you get some form of justification, why usually leads to because of this or that etc.

I my view, it actually disempowers your client. So, What and How are always better.

The GROW Model

The GROW model was originally developed by Graham Alexander and was then promoted and given more credence by Sir John Whitmore in his book "Coaching For Performance". It is probably the best-known coaching model in the UK. Many coach training programmes use this model as the framework for developing the coaching relationship.

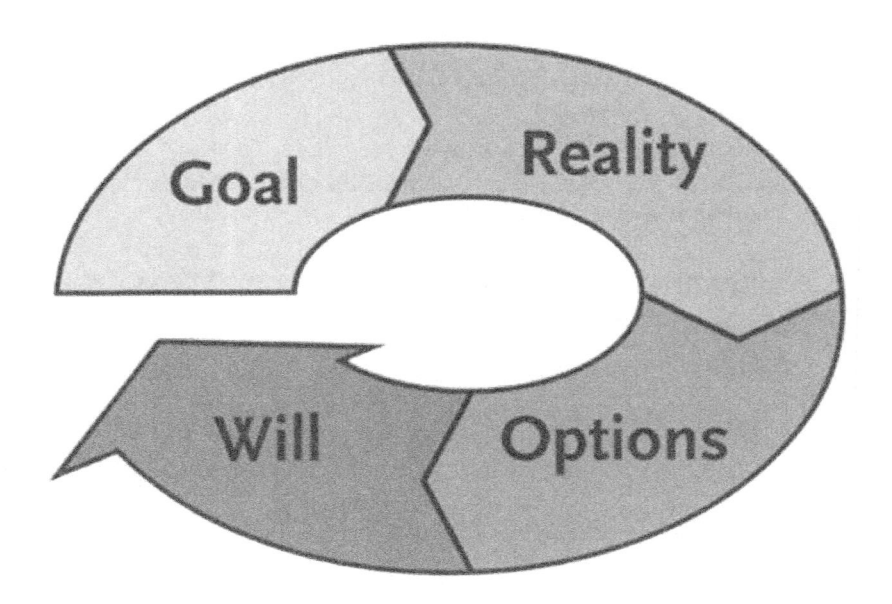

A 2002 study conducted by the Work Foundation and the School of Coaching revealed that 34% of respondents stated that they used the GROW model, one third cited they used a variety of models and the remaining third did not know what model or process was used in their coaching activities. So being one of the most popular coaching models we will spend a little extra time looking at it.

Goals: breaking things up, your way to mastery

We all recognize the importance of having goals. And yet, for most of us achieving goals is a mountain of a challenge.

If you were to imagine that solving complex problems and achieving predictable results were part of a process, where do you think is the best place to start would be?

Would you start by trying to solve the big, much more complex challenge? Or would you perhaps focus on breaking the complex problem into achievable mini goals?

www.ukcpd.co.uk

Knowing how to establish goals is a key part of achievement. A good strategy is by learning to create SMART goals - specific, measurable, attainable, relevant and time bound.

Specific: few people understand how setting specific goals works. It's very easy to be vague, we try to improve our "focus" for example when this can mean many things. It's much more effective to work on specific actions e.g., tossing the ball correctly if we're looking to improve our free throw

Measurable: how do you know that you're making progress? If you can't measure and receive clear feedback against your established goals, improvement is at best good luck.

Attainable: part of breaking things down into mini goals, is that it makes it easier to complete much bigger goals. When we work and complete many attainable goals, our success builds up and our ability to solve more complex problems improves.

Relevant: goals should be established to improve behaviours or processes rather than outcomes. We can't really control the outcome, but we can continually learn a great deal about new and vital behaviours that improve our outcomes.

Time-bound: goals have a habit of not getting done if there's no timeframe behind them. If we're not accountable to getting things done in a certain time, we tend to put things off; search for ways for keeping yourself accountable.

GOAL Focused Questions

- What is the goal of this discussion?
- What form of outcome are you seeking by the end of this session?
- How far and how detailed do you expect to get in this session?

- What is the subject matter or the issue on which you would like to work?
- What do you want to achieve (short and long term?)
- Is it an end goal or a performance goal?
- If it is an end goal what is a performance goal related to it?
- When do you want to achieve it by?
- How is that positive, challenging, attainable, and measurable?

What's The REALITY of the Current Situation?

The second step is figuring out where you stand. When you created your goals, you established them to be realistic based on the SMART formula.

This second step in the GROW coaching model, consists in determining where you are in respect to your goals. In other words, you constantly evaluate how you've progressed in your abilities, motivation, skills and knowledge taking your goals as a rule of measurement.

Coaching is effective because it's very hard to determine what you may need help or further training in by yourself. You frequently need an outside point of view to get a good idea of where you may need to improve.

You could also ask the following questions:

- What is the present situation in more detail?
- What and how great is you concern about it?
- Who is affected by the issue other than you?
- Who knows about your desire to do something about it?
- How much control do you personally have over the outcome?
- Who else has some control over it, and how much?

- What is happening now? (what, when, where, how much?)
- What action steps have you taken on it so far?
- What results is that producing?
- What stopped you from doing more?
- What obstacles will need to be overcome on the way?
- What if any, internal obstacles or personal resistances do you have taking action?
- What is happening both internally and externally?
- What are the major constraints to finding a way forward?
- What resources do you already have? Skill, time, enthusiasm, money support.
- What other resources will you need? Where will you get them from?
- What is really the issue here, the nub of the issue or the bottom line?

Time to look at what OPTIONS the client has

The third step is about figuring out what to do. What are the many possible options the client has for solving a problem? Among the many options possible, which one would they choose?

It helps if you begin by understanding what their unique strengths are. When you understand what your strengths are, it makes choosing options simpler.

You're more likely to achieve growth and do better by learning how to use your strengths and you'll probably feel happier as well.

Some useful questions include the following:

- What are all the different ways you could approach this issue?
- What else could you do?
- Make a list of all the alternatives, large or small, complete or partial solutions.
- What would you do if you had more time, a larger budget or you were the boss?
- What if…?
- Would you like to add a suggestion from me?
- What are the benefits and costs of each?
- Which would give the best result?
- Which of these solutions appeals to you most, or feels best to you?
- Which would give you the most satisfaction?

What WILL you commit to doing?

The final step is the driving force of the process, anything that needs to get done, requires some sort of action. It also needs energy to keep things moving. The final step in this model is to get your client to commit to specific action.

In so doing, your client can establish his or her motivation.

- What are you going to do?
- Which option/options do you choose?
- To what extent does this meet your objectives?
- How will you measure success?
- When precisely are you going to start and finish each action plan step?
- Will this meet your goal?
- What obstacles could you face to hinder you taking these steps?
- What personal resistance do you have to taking any of these steps?

- How will you overcome any obstacles/eliminate internal and external barriers?
- Who needs to know what your plans are?
- What support do you need and from whom?
- How will you get that support?
- How committed are you on a one to ten scales on the likelihood of carrying out this action?
- What prevents this being a 10?
- What could you do to alter/raise your commitment closer to 10?
- Is there anything else you want to talk about now or are we finished?

Keep in mind, that these steps aren't sequential, they're not meant to be followed one after the other rather, the key is to remain flexible, so you can review your perceptions, make adjustments, course correct, and tune things up a little if needed.

This way, you make it a constant process of improvement. One that's grounded on the clients' values, uniqueness and wants.

In essence, the GROW coaching model is a very simple, powerful and effective tool to have in your coaching toolbox.

The APROCESS Coaching Model

This is the NLP model I mentioned before. In NLP there is the idea of "Well Formed Outcomes" (Goals) it takes the ideas in many coaching or goal setting models and creates a structure that really makes the difference; the "well Formedness" is the key to success.

Why are 'well formed' outcomes important? Deciding on a goal or outcome is the starting point of any developmental and change process. Before investing energy and time it makes sense to ensure that the 'What' 'How' and, yes even the 'Why' has been well explored, checked out and specified.

Quite often wishes stay as wishes because there has been no systematic application of the 'How' to achieve a goal or 'What' specifically do I want and it is easy to forget the 'Why' of 'why is this important' in the correct context.

The APROCESS model helps to transform vague and ill-defined outcomes into outcomes, which are well formed.

Aim: Ok, What do you want? What do you REALLY want? (a specific goal for the future) How is this new or different to what I have now?

Positive: How is this, a good thing for you? What's the "pay off"? A one sentence that says it all. We are looking for the why, why the client is going to do this?

Resources: What "stuff" do you need to achieve this goal? By stuff or resources, we mean, people, knowledge, money, skills etc. be clear what exactly it is that they will need to accomplish this goal, break it down into small steps.

Own Part: Is this goal really theirs, explain how they "own" this, how they will be able to maintain ownership, motivation etc?

Consequences: What will happen if they do not attain this goal? Be clear about the "pain" that they will experience.

What will happen when they do? Be clear about the pleasure that they will enjoy, ask, what will you see, hear and feel?

Evidence: How will they know they are making progress? What will they see, hear and feel? At the halfway mark etc …

Anything Else? – this is a great question, use it often during a session.

Start (time frame) When are you going to take the first step? What date would you want to be halfway, what date are you going to set for accomplishment of this goal?

Steps (First): What's the first step? Who can you call right now? What can you do today that will start the process?

Ok, so the key thing to remember with the START and committing to a Time Frame is that it's so easy to procrastinate and think I will get round to this soon . . .or one day etc.

Be clear, ask your client to write down a start date, this is a way of making the goal a reality, and getting some momentum and strong commitment to taking action.

Ask your client to, think ahead, set a target for a halfway marker, encourage your client to set a stake in the ground of your future life, taking into consideration all of the information they have put together as you went through this process with them.

And now, the end game, when is the date they wish to realise your goal and to really be enjoying your personal success? Again, be clear, look ahead into your future and hammer in a big bright stake in their timeline, the date that they will have achieved their outcome.

Other Useful Questions For Outcomes

- What's the heart of the matter?
- What's the real issue?
- What is stopping you?
- How is that a problem for you?
- What will that do for you?

Example: The APROCESS Coaching Model

Here we have an example of The APROCESS Coaching Model being used, this is a transcript taken from a LIVE training session at UKCPD.

The APROCESS Coaching Model Transcript

Coach: So, Lucy, hello. How are you doing?

Client: Yeah. Good. Thank you.

Coach: Good. What would you like from today's session?

Client: I would like to get to a point with my blog that I can attend Blogtacular on the 18th of June and be really proud of the content I'm delivering.

Coach: Wow you will have to say that one more time.

Client: Okay. I'm working. I've got a blog and - - -, I'm going to a conference called Blogtacular, and that's where a lot of bloggers meet. And it's a big networking and you get a lot of exposure. So, you meet a lot of people there. Um, and for me, it's a massive networking opportunity for my next step.

And at the moment, my blog isn't as great as it could be the content isn't regular. And I want to. Get to a point where I've, I can be really proud of my blog, walk through that door and be really happy with what someone will just go straight onto my blog and look at it while I'm, while they're there. And I want them to feel connected to me and want to hatefully work with me in the future.

Coach: Okay. So, I've got a couple of questions for you if I may. Uh, well, the first one, would it help If I knew what you blogged about.

Client: Yeah!

Coach: Okay.

Client: So, I blog about live cultivating and living a creative life.

Coach: Wow, cultivating and living a creative life.

Client: Yeah. So, growing creative life, basically,

Coach: Like, we're doing now?

Client: yea.

Coach: Okay. So, I've got something of context.

Client: Yeah.

Coach: And you want to attend this Blogtacular, have I said that, right?

Client: Yeah.

Coach: That's not a real word. All right. Log in, in June. Did you say in June? Okay. So, what's your actual outcome for this session? Is it planning a trip to Blogtacular or is it something around what you're actually doing now with your blog?

Client: So, it's doing something with my blog. It's getting. Okay. To a place where I'm really proud of the content, that's regular content going on there. And the level of content is starting to maybe move towards my kind of coaching piece as well as the stuff that I currently write about.

Coach: Okay. So that's a lot of aims, so tell me, what's this about really if you attend Blogtacular, and you're sort of networking and you're sort of hanging out with the cool

www.ukcpd.co.uk

kids, I can use that. What's that all about? What's that doing for you?

Client: That is making me feel part of the community. So, I went last year, and it changed, everything it meant I came on this course, cause I said to everyone, I'm going to be a coach. And everyone's like, you'd be really good coach. You should do that. And so, I wanted to find the right course I found the right course, and this year I want to go back and say, I am a coach, and this is what I'm doing.

Coach: Right.

Client: Yeah.

Coach: So, going back to what you said before, I understand your motivation now. What's -- what's the one sentence version of what you actually want?

Client: To have a blog I'm proud of.

Coach: To have a blog you're proud of.

Client: Yeah.

Coach: Okay. To have a blog that you're proud of, um, what resources are required for you or need anybody, but let's concentrate on you to have a blog that one would be proud of per se.

Client: Time, to write and photograph, um, sources mainly to upgrade my phone, but I don't think so. I've con I can take photos with the camera I've got on my phone at the moment. That's fine. I might actual cameras, um, ideas and a plan of content. So, I want to get to a point where I'm writing weekly content at the moment.

It's quite sporadic and I'm not. I haven't really, I can't, there's nothing on there at the moment that is sort of saying, yeah, she's really, she's a serious blogger, whereas a serious blogger writes what they write one maybe once a day, or like a couple of times a week. I want to do just once a week that would do me fine find and have a proper regular schedule of blogging.

Coach: So, let me just check this out. Is that the real outcome? To be a regular writer and post.

Client: Yea, because it gives you kudos in terms of like, yeah, you can, you are sticking to it. I know I can stick to some stuff, but I don't seem to be second to this. Um, and to have that there, it sort of shows that I'm when I go to Blogtacular I want to go in there and I want to make an impression and to make an impression you need to, you need to be a good blogger, you know, you need to be regular, regular blogger because if you don't post, most people are like, so I, you know, I hear it if you only post like once a month, because it's not kind of yeah. In the community that I'm part of. Um, am I read a lot of blogs? There is sort of an achievement status of yeah.

I'm working through there. There are people that are doing things that I don't want to do, like working with sponsors for me, it's all about the content and it's building my business. So, I'm saying, trying to set my sights and get to Blogtacular and then to let something blossom at Blogtacular.

Coach: Right?

Client: Yeah.

Coach: So, the real outcome that we're going to work on today, if I'm right, is you blogging once a week?

Client: Yeah, that is right. Yeah.

Coach: The reason for this, the positive payoff is you will be taken seriously by your peer group. When you turn up and going, hey, bloggers, check me out. Yeah, I'm doing what I said I was going to do. Okay. So, if I ask you the resource question again, what's required for you to be able to sit and write at least once a week.

Client: The time to sit at my desk, I have my stations set up. I'm really happy with. I've got my Mac. Don't like max, but I've got my Mac. I've got my Mac. I've got, I have got a planner, which I'm not using. Um, but I love my planner when I do use it. It feels very motivational, but I'm not actually writing in it.

Coach: Yeah.

Client: At the moment. So, a list, a list of blog posts I'm feel really excited by that. Really speak to my kind of subject area and people will be quite engaged with.

Coach: Ok, of those resources. You've mentioned a few things sort of stand out to me, time planner.

Client: Yeah.

Coach: I'll discount the Mac as they are real computers, as you know, (audience laughs) so time planner and then a list of specific topics that appeal to your subject area.

Client: Yeah. Yeah.

Coach: Okay, so of those resources, which do you have right now? That you can point to and say, yep, that's in the bag.

Client: I've got, the planner is empty.

Coach: Right.

Client: And I've got a pen to write and, um, I've got a partial list that I started at the beginning of the year, that I do turn back to and go, oh yeah. I've actually written that book about my top 16 books for 2016. Good job. But you kind of wanted to write that in January. Um, so yeah, so I'm quite that I only pasted that two weeks ago and it was a great post.

Coach: I believe you, you seem excited .

Client: It was really delayed. So, yeah. So, I have got a list that I could turn back to, which has got my sort of topic areas.

Coach: Right.

Client: I did brainstorm at the beginning of the year, when I was on supposed to be doing one post a week.

Coach: Yes. As I'm going to ask you again, this mythical list, does it exist in the sense of you look at it and you go right this week, I'm going to do.

Client: No, I haven't put a day next, like a date next to it. It's just a list of subject areas.

Coach: So, a list of subject areas that exist that you can look at and go, I'm going to do that one this time I could pick. Right. So, so that's not the thing that's missing.

Client: No.

Coach: So, let's go back to time,

Client: Time. Yeah.

Coach: Tell me about that.

Client: Time's a bit tricky at the moment.

Coach: Is it?

Client: Yeah. it's really hard for this because we've got obviously a certain number of weeks left and I want to put my all into it. I'm also at that crucial six month wedding point in time, um, where I'm having to make some quite big decisions that are quite time consuming.

And then work is also being busier at the normal thing, quite quiet at the beginning of the year, when I thought of this brilliant one blog post a week plan. And yeah, and I tried to fit in exercise as well for the wedding dress for the wedding, all of that. Right. So, so it's being pushed down the priority list, but I want it to kind of note it up cause it's as important.

Coach: Right? Can we cancel the wedding?

Client: No. No.

Coach: Are you sure?

Client: Yeah.

Coach: Right. Can you cancel completing the course?

Client: No, no.

Coach: That's not going to happen, is it? Can we cancel work?

Client: No.

Coach: No. Okay. So, it seems to me, we have to do something else. Right? How long does it take to write a blog? I mean, there's a dissertation. Is it like five lines or how long does it take?

Client: So, I can sometimes write a blog post on the train in my 12 minute change to any if I've been starting to think about it beforehand, or sometimes moments comes around. I'm like, right. Yeah. Get that down. And then it takes some refinement. So probably about two hours, as well as having the time doing a photo.

Cause I have to put a photo with the words otherwise, who reads blog posts without a photo.

Coach: That sound ghastly (audience laughs) - - Right? How many words? Roughly.

Client: I would say let's just put four paragraph four or five paragraphs. **Coach:** So, five paragraphs.

Client: Yeah.

Coach: Okay. So just have to kind of a sense. Yeah. Uh, two hours with a bit of sort of polishing and a suitable photograph.

Client: Yeah.

Coach: Right. Okay. Looking at your schedule. Imagine if it was here right now. Yeah, that's right. Um, what day of the week is probably the best.

www.ukcpd.co.uk

Client: So, writing can be done in my train journeys, which happens every day of the week. Monday to Friday.

Coach: No, hang on a second.

Client: What day do I have to post it? - - Sorry ..

Coach: Writing can be done when I'm on the train, but is it going to be done when you're on the train?

Client: No, not every day because I like a very journey.

Coach: I dare say, so we'll go again to having a day, what day would be best given that's the start of the process. And then there's the refining and then there's the getting of the photograph. And then there's the posting part.

Client: Yeah. I probably choose today Tuesday.

Coach: Tuesday.

Client: Yeah. Because on Monday I'm trying to do a bit of exercise, more exercise than my walk. So, Tuesday I've got a gap there there's a gap. Yeah. Right. And then I've got plenty of time to write that.

Coach: So,

Client: So, I'd like to ideally post on a Saturday or Sunday. Right because I could do my photography over a weekend because I have daylight because in the evenings I come home from work and there's no daylight to take a photo, a good photo, and a good photo is important. So, Tuesday,

Coach: So, Tuesday on the train perhaps, or just wandering around, you're going to start writing, start writing on your phone or laptop.

Client: Yeah. No, on my phone yeah. Evernote app.

Coach: Yep. I'm familiar with that. Okay. Um, then what will happen?

Client: On Tuesday? On my train day, I tend to email it to myself to go, don't forget to post it. Right. Okay. So, from Evernote, I'll email it to my email account.

Coach: Yes. Okay.

Client: I flag it in my email account.

Coach: Then what will happen then?

Client: Then I should do some editing.

Coach: Should...? What will you do? I will.

Client: I will edit

Coach: What day?

Client: Probably Saturday. So, I get the words out and then I like to ruminate on that a little bit and decide if actually is that what I want to put out there? Yeah. Um, and then Saturday morning I can get up quite early on a Saturday. Yeah. And it can sometimes be posted by 10 o'clock. Yeah. When I'm in a good schedule.

Coach: So, so just for the sake of my understanding and yours, your outcome here is to wright on a Tuesday.

Client: Yeah

Coach: Email it to yourself on a Tuesday.

Client: Yeah.

Coach: Reflect and ruminate on it for the rest of the week, and on a Saturday, shine it all up. Attach a suitable photograph and post. What time on Saturday?

Client: I can get up at, at half past seven, make a cup of tea and just do it. And so, I can get it done before the day begins. And that fits in with other stuff going on.

Coach: So, who's in control of all of the, all of that process, all of that outcome, because it's fair few steps here.

Client: Yeah, I am because no one writes my content. I do my photos, my train journey.

Coach: Yeah. Okay. So, what are the consequences of not doing this? Given you've mentioned before you had said thing and it didn't happen.

Client: So, I think there's, I think I feel that I won't have achieved what I really want to do before June, and if I can start if I can start now, I can look really good or I can look an average blogger when I get there. Um, and I'm not in that high class of bloggers.

I don't want to be in that. I want to be in the undercurrent of, um, of people. So, I know that I will fit into that and have great conversations and learn stuff while I'm there.

Coach: Okay. So, the consequences of getting this in place every single week,

Client: This is the basic bit,

Coach: this is the basic bit. So once this is up and running and you have, you know, put this strategy into, uh, into practice and it's a regular thing Tuesdays on the train writing ruminating Saturday mornings, getting up early polishing photograph posting.

Client: Yeah.

Coach: Tell me. What will that do for you? Consequences wise of success. If we build that as a success, what will that mean to you? Do for you enable …

Client: It will enable me to have a set of people at Blogtacular that I'll meet that are now about to tap into when I start my business. So, um, from previous experience of last year, I've got a handful of people that I am regularly looking at blogs, liking their posts. They're like my stuff. And there's a bit of, kind of give and take there. And I know if I've built that a new set, an extra set of people that I've connected with. When I get to that point of wanting to trial my creative workshops in retreat, I'll have my captive audience that can. Know me know that I post regularly and I'm doing it really well. And I've got some really authentic content that takes a lot of thought that some people don't have authentic content, but I know I do. And that's why I spent quite a lot of time on it, but they'll come back. They want to come to my retreat and then they'll blog about it.

And I'll have my bit of marketing that I know will work for the audience that I'm looking for. So, it's really important to get it done,

Coach: I believe you; it sounds pretty compelling.

Client: It's really important.

Coach: How will you know that you've achieved this new habit, which is really what we're talking about of Tuesdays ruminating, Saturdays go, how will you know what…?

Client: I will know because over weekend my blog paste traffic will be over 100 people. Cause there'll be a nice spike in my graph. Um, on the side of my blog I've got the months and months of the year and they'll be four in each one. So, four posts each month. That's what I like.

Coach: Okay. Uh, anything else that would indicate success.

Client: I think I may have a few more Instagram followers on Instagram and I'd hope to have a couple of comments, but people don't tend to comment anymore, but I think, um, I'll have growing traffic or maybe a few more in the week. You'll see everything. I'll see all my graphs and behind the scenes of my blog.

Coach: What will you hear?

Client: I'll hear, You can do it. Yeah. Yeah. You could. I think that's the thing that moment I'm like, ah, I feel a bit of a fraud walking in to Blogtacular going. Yeah. I read my blog for since 2011. (Client get emotional .)

Client, (sounding quite emotional) I did not expect this to happen. sorry, I don't want to be a fraud because I want to make it work. And this is my one point. I know I can get my audience. I don't do the most basic thing that is writing a post every week, which is pretty goddamn, basic the

www.ukcpd.co.uk

world of blogging. You're not going to take it seriously and I'm not going to get that marketing on each of my course.

Coach: Yeah.

Client: My entire plan. Yeah. And my book and my back, there's a whole bunch of things. There's a whole bunch of stuff there. So, it's walking into that room. There's a lot of people there that really know what they're doing, and I want to be one of those people that knows what they're doing.

Coach: Right. So, when you got to start?

Client: I'm going to start on Monday, Tuesday.

Coach: Tuesday!

Client: Well, I've already done. Kat helped me get my pictures done this morning so I could actually post something already. This week.

Coach: Okay. So, we'll start this Tuesday would be my new post.

Client: Yep.

Coach: So, the following Saturday, which is Easter Saturday, is that right? **Client:** Yeah, that's fine.

Coach: You're up and go.

Client: Yep. I'm taking my laptop.

Coach: Okay. How many weeks before this new idea becomes a habit and a ritual that that's what you do every Tuesday on the train every Saturday, posting?

Client: I think six weeks, because I've got over that first month. So, I did a first month in January. Yay. But then it all went wrong in February. So, if I can get to six weeks and get that point of like, yeah, I'm into that next month, then that will show me that I can really do it.

Coach: Okay. So, thinking about that strategy, now, what you're going to do the first step is what?

Client: The first step is to sit on the train and open Evernote on Tuesday. **Coach:** Yeah.

Client: And write something.

Coach: I'm going to ask you a difficult question.

Client: Okay.

Coach: Knowing you as you do. And you're spinning a lot of plates, jobs, weddings, courses.

Client: Yeah.

Coach: How might this go horribly wrong?

Client: How could it go wrong? If don't have the discipline on Tuesdays to do it, but I know I've got a bit of wiggle room on my Wednesdays, Thursdays and Friday morning. If I don't do on the Tuesday, I have got the rest of that week. But the Saturday I do love doing that blog post in the morning on a Saturday.

Cause it kind of kick-starts my weekend.

Coach: Yeah. So, so you mentioned the word discipline. So, it was an interesting word.

Client: Yeah. We don't always like disciplined, but actually it's a good thing. Client: Yea, but I like discipline

Coach: Yeah, I can see you do. Yes. Um, how can you reward yourself on that Saturday by pressing that button, what would help you to go, post - reward that would help you go. Yes, I'm making, I'm just kind of saying yes. I'm acknowledging my real progress of developing a new strategy habit.

Client: I think I've got to do something that will be visual for me, so I can, apart from the screens, I think it needs to be at my desk.

Coach: Yeah.

Client: So, I've got my wall of like inspirational stuff I have in front of me. I think I could create something for each month. Just a very simple little chart where I'm sticking something on it. Like her child. I go and get myself an ice coffee from the coffee shop. Something like that.

Coach: Yeah, maybe it's all of the senses, smelling and testing the coffee.

Client: Maybe it's going to coffee. Number One. After I've posted. That's a treat. Cause I don't go and do that because yeah. I may go a little bit of cake.

Coach: What cake specifically.

Client: Well, there's carrot cake

Coach: It's got carrot in it; it's got to be healthy. Yes. All right. Would it help if I was to email you on a Friday to say good luck for tomorrow. It being done Saturday, right.

Client: That could be, don't forget to get your ass in gear.

Coach: Yeah. Well, I might use other words, but yeah. Yeah. Okay.

Client: Yeah. I think that would, yeah. So definitely set my alarm.

Coach: Well, yeah. Okay. So, Tuesday. Maybe Wednesday or Tuesdays the target then some ruminating.

Client: Yep. Tuesdays the start.

Coach: Then Saturday. Well, Friday email saying good luck. I'm looking forward to yeah, because you can give me the blog address. Yeah.

Client: Yeah. Oh God!

Coach: Well, you can follow mine and I'll follow you and then you'll get up Saturday. You'll post. Yep. And I'll be waiting for it. Yeah, she does it. Yeah. And then I'll know you're in the coffee shop. Eating cake.

Client: Yeah. So, I need to do it in the morning.

Coach: Yeah. Okay.

Client: That's what I'd like to do in the morning.

Coach: Right - Excellent.

Client: In the morning on Saturday.

Coach: We're good to go then.

Client: Yeah.

Coach: Wow. I'm looking forward to reading it.

Client: Thank you.

So, lots to take from this session. You can see the value of the model in guiding the client and chucking down for the first stated goal to something that was way more specific and actually measurable.

One other thing that stand out for me now is just how much the client speaks compared to the coach, the client is doing all the work.

Chapter Seven: Developing Your Practice

How will you position your service / practice?

Some coaches position themselves as straightforward coaches, offering all kinds of coaching.

Others decide to specialise. There is no right or wrong answer. In fact, many general coaches also specialise in one area.

But clients are attracted by specialisms. If you want to buy a pair of shoes, you'd probably go to a shoe shop, rather than a department store, on the grounds that the shoe shop knew more about shoes and had a bigger range.

If you intend to specialise, you should do so in an area that fascinates you. Otherwise, you won't bring the dynamism, focus and concentration that marks out the good coach.

So, you should decide what kind of coaching service you intend to offer. Experience will help you develop a better idea of the kind of coaching you feel most confident about.

Here are some of the main specialisms:

Small Business Coach

A huge number of small businesspeople trade on the Internet, and many are working in a solitary manner. They don't have anyone they can express their fears and anxieties to. And they need someone who they can talk to about the business.

If you have some experience of business, you can offer your services as a small business coach. You don't have to be an expert in their business; you merely have to have the characteristics of a good coach. That is to say, you should be sympathetic, challenging, questioning, and interested in your client.

Relationships Coach

Human beings seem to need a mate, a best friend, a lover. And often these are all rolled into one. And when the relationship isn't working, it causes us grief. No wonder so many clients want to discuss their relationships.

Relationships coaches can discuss their client's relationship with their spouse, their children or their boss. And for the millions of single people who are dating, relationships are a continuous source of concern. The conversations and concerns seen on the TV series, 'Sex and the city' are echoed in the telephone conversations of coaches around the world.

They ask questions like,

- Doesn't he fancy me?
- Should I ask her out?
- Should I find a new partner?

The coach has no answers to give, of course. The coach merely lets the client come to a conclusion, while at the same time encouraging them to be pro-active.

Career Coach

Coaches find themselves discussing careers a lot. This is because work is uppermost on many clients' minds. So, if this is an area that interests you, you should consider specialising in it.

As a personal work coach can help people seek promotion or decide whether to change career. Or you can help them revise their CV or resume. In other cases, you can help the client improve their work-life balance, by working less frenetically. Or they may decide to opt out of the rat race, and down-size.

Business Coach

As a coach hired by an organization, you can help employees to be more effective in their job. You could train them to be better presenters, or to manage time better. You can also help people to get on better with their colleagues. There is a range of consulting-type activities that the coach can offer to businesses.

Working Mothers Coach

To see how one coach has focused on the 'working mother' area, take a look at www.bluesuitmom.com. Working mothers suffer from more stress and possibly guilt, so they are good candidates for coaching.

Health and Fitness Coach*

With millions of people overweight or obese, large numbers of clients know they need to lose weight, take up exercise, and eat better. You can help clients devise a program that will help them achieve that. It goes without saying that you have to be slim, fit and healthy to do this kind of work.

Addictions Coach*

Think of all those people indulging in tobacco, alcohol, barbiturates and other drugs. Many of them want to quit but need someone to help them through the difficult change- over period. You could be there to mentor them.

You will need to add additional training and experience in these specific areas if you wish to focus your practice in this area. Individuals working in these areas are often licensed, and you will need to be clear not to step into an area that is regulated i.e., psychotherapy / counselling.

Potential Sources of Work

As a coach, you can get work from several main sources. We have listed the sources of work in roughly the right order of importance for a new coaching practice.

Your website

Networking

Leaflet drops

Seminars

PR

Referrals from existing clients

Advertising

Businesses

Your Website

If you haven't got a website, get one now. Why'? Because your website is the 21st century equivalent of the brochure. It can tell the visitor everything they need to know about your service. So, by the time they email or phone you, all the selling has been done. A good website should leave potential client with no questions to ask.

When you hand someone a business card, they will see you have a website, and will go to it. The website also saves you having to send out expensive brochures, and it's available instantly and round the clock, whereas a brochure can take days to get to the recipient.

There are lots of low-cost options for building a website, from WordPress to WIX etc.

Your website should be clear and set out some key content including:

- An explanation about coaching
- Your services
- Useful free information, such as articles
- Unsolicited testimonials
- Your prices
- An e-book for sale
- One or more free articles that the reader has to send for
- Your photograph

Below we discuss some of these points.

Making Your Website Work

You should have an online form that lets people sign up easily for a newsletter, or other download such as an e-book. Either learn to do this yourself or get a local web builder to do it for you.

Set up a STRIPE or PayPal account that lets you take payment on your website This saves people having to send you cheques or phone you up with their credit card details.

Get your text written correctly on the web page. For example, avoid excessive use of the word "I" on the website. Spend more time talking about 'you'. Here is ***how not to*** do it:

I coach private individuals by phone. Typically, clients have 45 min calls weekly, with support between calls by e-mail. I work with people to develop and enrich their lives. I've had a number of specialism's, but I do other types of coaching too. (If you contact me and I don't feel I'm the coach for you, I'll help you find your ideal match).

I had a corporate background in HR working with people to get I the best from their careers or find a new one. I've continued this kind of work into my private practice. I'm a qualified Myers Briggs practitioner too! I am a creative person and have released a number of compilations of my compositions. I've been through various artistic ups and' downs and now I am interested in working with people on unlocking latent talents and helping established artists unblock and find new directions.

Blog

Your website should contain at least one free article. Why? Because it sells you as an expert in the subject area.

Your E-Book

If you browse the net looking at other coaches' websites, you'll see that some of them are offering e-books. These are self-help manuals either on general or specialist coaching subjects.

The advantage of these e-books is that they earn you money while you sleep. Or give them away from free when potential clients register for your newsletter.

Networking

You should constantly be networking — that means simply meeting people who might need your services. In turn, that means being active in the local community. But only get involved in activities that you enjoy, or it will seem a chore and you may stop doing it.

Remember that your contacts may not need your services, but they may know someone who does. The more you talk about coaching, the greater your chances of finding clients.

Leaflet Drop

If you intend to do face-to-face coaching, put leaflets through the letter boxes of homes in your area. Potential clients are more- likely to be found in the better parts of your area. People who live in run-down council estates are unlikely to have the money to pay.

You can do this in several ways:

- Put the leaflets through people's letterbox yourself.
- Pay someone else to do it (perhaps a young person you trust).
- Ask a newsagent to deliver a leaflet with the paper round.
- Write to people's names and addresses from the electoral list (at the library).
- Ask the post office to deliver the mail as 'unaddressed mail', which is at a cheaper rate than normal post.

Seminars

There are two kinds of seminar, those that you charge people to attend, and those that you provide free of charge.

Paid-for Seminars

You can run paid-for seminars if you are well known as a coach, which is possibly unlikely at this stage of your career. So, you might want to leave this until you're better known.

Motivational speakers can also charge for their seminars. Again, if you aren't highly skilled at public speaking, you might want to leave this for a later time.

Free Seminars

Free seminars are a great way to get business. They are simple to organise, the point of a free seminar is that it attracts people who subsequently become your one-to-one clients. Consider it as a free taster for your services.

www.ukcpd.co.uk

Using PR to Get Business

You may wish to consider writing a press release and sending it to the local press. PR can bring a good response, if the paper bothers to print your phone number or address.

In it, you can tell the world that you have set up as a coach. You might include one thing newsworthy at the start, such as a free initial consultation. You could offer to write a series of articles about how people can be their own coach, about improving their work-life balance, about achieving more from their life, and so on.

Your Own Newspaper Column

A good PR opportunity is to have your own coaching column in your local p newspaper or magazine. Write to the Editor and suggest that you run a column.

Every week, you would answer two or three readers' queries. Though the work would be unpaid, you would get invaluable free publicity. In time, you will build up a series of article for your website or an e-book.

Gaining Referrals

In the medium term, referrals will possibly be your biggest source of work. It can be irritating to have spent money promoting yourself and then a prospect rings you are saying, "Harry mentioned you're a coach".

But you can't rely on referrals, so you should treat them as the pleasant surprise they are and keep promoting yourself. And in the short term, when you are setting up your practice, you won't get many.

www.ukcpd.co.uk

But you should always ask a client if they know anyone who might benefit from coaching. Consider the following:

- An elderly lady who wants someone to talk to. She will know other such people.
- A small businessperson you coach will know other small business people.
- Someone you coach attends a local church and mentions your name to other people in the congregation.

Offering an inducement for referring a friend (e.g., free pen) is less suitable in coaching than it is in other markets.

But referrals are still possible. When you get to the end of a coaching program, ask your client if they know anyone who might like coaching. Give the client some cards which they can give to a friend.

Advertising

Advertising is often money wasted. But you may decide to try it. A few pointers are:

Don't simply advertise in your local newspaper, unless it is clustered with other similar kinds of services. Otherwise, people will overlook it.

Consider the smaller, less mainstream media first. For example, consider putting postcards in shop windows, or advertising in parish or local club magazines.

You should draw up a list of all the media in your area. You can find out the media through personal experience and through research. Your research will come from looking on newsagent's stands and through looking in the library.

www.ukcpd.co.uk

THE MEDIA

For a coach, the media can be divided into the following types:

Community and Parish Publications

These publications are the least professional in appearance, but often the most effective. They are read by people in a small area. You can often buy quite a big space, say I/4 page, for a modest cost.

Local Newspaper

The local press will include:

Paid-for papers, whether a weekly paper or a daily paper (or both).

Free-sheets. These are pushed through the letterbox free of charge.

Writing an Ad

Your ad should tell the reader about the service you supply. It should contain your name and telephone number, plus web address, email address, and finally the address if there is room. Don't make the ad too crowded, or it won't stand out.

Your ad can either be Display (this has a box around it, is usually larger, and is more expensive), or Classified (which has no box).

Response Rates

You can expect a 1% to 5% response rate from mailing or leaflet drops. That means you get one to five replies for every 100 letters you mail. So, you have to mail enough letters to get a good response.

For companies, you can do telesales. Telesales can be four times as effective as mailing. In other words, phoning might get you four to twenty responses for every one hundred decision makers contacted.

The outcome of your letters or phone calls is a meeting. Some clients don't fix meetings unless they have work in mind. Others will fix a meeting if they think they will need your services in the near future.

You can expect to convert around one in three meetings into actual work. This means that you have to mail 300 people to be sure of getting one job. When you get clients, make sure you hold to them. It is easier and cheaper to get repeat business from an existing client than to find a new one.

Review:

So, I trust the content of this introductory book has been insightful and useful as you either consider becoming a coach or you are already in training and working towards your qualification and starting to develop your coaching practice.

The UK College of Personal Development has a range of coaching qualifications, both Professional and Academic.

Visit our website:

UK COLLEGE OF PERSONAL DEVELOPMENT

www.ukcpd.co.uk

Printed in Great Britain
by Amazon